Ritual: A Very Short Introduction

VERY SHORT INTRODUCTIONS are for anyone wanting a stimulating and accessible way in to a new subject. They are written by experts and have been translated into more than 40 different languages.

The series began in 1995 and now covers a wide variety of topics in every discipline. The VSI library now contains more than 400 volumes—a Very Short Introduction to everything from Indian philosophy to psychology and American History—and continues to grow in every subject area.

Very Short Introductions available now:

For more information visit our website

www.oup.com/vsi/

Barry Stephenson

RITUAL

A Very Short Introduction

OXFORD

UNIVERSITY PRESS

Oxford University Press is a department of the
University of Oxford. It furthers the University's objective
of excellence in research, scholarship, and education
by publishing worldwide.

Oxford   New York

Auckland   Cape Town   Dar es Salaam   Hong Kong   Karachi
Kuala Lumpur   Madrid   Melbourne   Mexico City   Nairobi
New Delhi   Shanghai   Taipei   Toronto

With offices in

Argentina   Austria   Brazil   Chile   Czech Republic   France   Greece
Guatemala   Hungary   Italy   Japan   Poland   Portugal   Singapore
South Korea   Switzerland   Thailand   Turkey   Ukraine   Vietnam

Oxford is a registered trade mark of Oxford University Press
in the UK and certain other countries.

Published in the United States of America by
Oxford University Press
198 Madison Avenue, New York, NY 10016

Library of Congress Cataloging-in-Publication Data
Stephenson, Barry.
Ritual : a very short introduction / Barry Stephenson.
pages cm
Includes bibliographical references and index.
ISBN 978-0-19-994352-4 (pbk.)
1. Ritual.   I. Title.
BL600.S735   2015
390—dc23   2014028719

3 5 7 9 8 6 4 2

Printed in Great Britain
by Ashford Colour Press Ltd, Gosport, Hants.
on acid-free paper

Contents

List of illustrations

Acknowledgments

Many people and organizations have provided me the opportunity to think, talk, and write about ritual. First and foremost is Ronald Grimes, whose contribution and commitment to the field of ritual studies is unparalleled. Tom Driver, Ute Hüsken, and Michael Houseman and have been wonderful to work with and to learn from. Axel Michaels, director of the Dynamics of Ritual Project at the University of Heidelberg, kindly invited me to several events during the time I was finding my feet in the world of ritual studies. My thanks go out to Oxford University Press. Nancy Toff and the editing team gave this book a thorough and much-needed edit; over the years Oxford has been very supportive of scholarship on ritual.

Introduction

Ritual, like language, tool use, symbolism, and music, is one of the constituent elements in the mix of what it means to be human. The cultural record reveals the persistence and pervasiveness of ritual. The archaeological record suggests that ritual was present at the dawn of humanity. The biological record shows that ritualization is a fundamental feature of animal behavior and contributes to evolutionary processes. To think about ritual, then, is to reflect on human nature, sociality, and culture.

Ritual is something we cannot avoid. Particular rituals may be more or less important to certain people or to certain societies or groups; a devout Catholic goes to Mass each day, and the Hopi discreetly invest enormous amounts of time, money, and energy in ritual activity throughout the year. But even if we do not consider ourselves ritual beings or our society ritually based, an encounter with ritual in the course of a lifetime is as sure as the rising and setting of the sun. Weddings, funerals, birthdays, inaugurations, graduations, festivals, parades, liturgies, the exchange of gifts—ritual permeates our social and personal life worlds. Ritual is formative of who we are, and we variously experience the rites and ceremonies that cross our paths as uplifting or boring, exploitive or empowering, creative or moribund. To think about ritual is to explore its place, power, and potential in our lives and our society.

For people raised in the modern and postmodern industrial West, ritual has been significantly marginalized from cultural and intellectual landscapes. Historically, the influence of Protestant and Enlightenment sensibilities led to a suspiciousness of ritual. Compared with science, reason, and the market, ritual has often been derided as a relatively ineffectual way of engaging the world. On the other hand, in recent critical discussions on the nature and project of modernity, ritual is making something of a comeback, and there is a newfound popular interest in the creative, critical, transformative potential of ritual. To think about ritual is to reflect on attitudes and assumptions informing the narrative arc of modernity.

A book on ritual, even a short one, ought to be able to answer the simple question, what is ritual? But, going out the gate we run in to a problem, one common to many fields of inquiry. Ritual has been studied from a variety of scholarly disciplines; as a result, it has been approached and defined in a myriad of ways. In a widely read encyclopedia article on "Ritual" published in 1968, the anthropologist Edmund Leach offered the somewhat dispiriting observation that "there is the widest possible disagreement as to how the word ritual should be used and how the performance of ritual should be understood." At that time, there was little consensus over what ritual is or what it does, if it does anything at all. In the decades since, matters have become, if anything, even more complicated. The waggling of bees and the genuflections of a priest; wearing the colors at a football match and the coffee break at the office; hospital birth and speaking in parliament; watching television and tending the garden; waiting at a bus stop in Wichita or attending Kabuki in Tokyo; birthday parties and Fourth of July parades—all this, and more, has been conceptualized, analyzed, and theorized as ritual. Ritual, it would seem, is all around us, and reflection on the nature, function, and place of ritual in society, culture, and religion has occupied many influential thinkers in the humanities and social sciences.

Broadly conceived, as it is in this book, "ritual" is not a particular kind of discrete action, but rather a quality of action potentially available across a spectrum of behavior. Ritual, as a metacategory, includes both religious and nonreligious rites, the traditional and the new, the prescribed and the improvised, the human and nonhuman, and rubs up against a number of other cultural domains, such as play, games, performance, and theater. If ritual is action, it is also an idea, something we think with, and our exploration will move back and forth between these two dimensions.

Ritual is first and foremost a doing. Like cooking or swimming or politics, we learn about ritual through the doing of it. But alongside ritual enactment, people also step back to think, write, and read about ritual—what you are doing now. This is not to polarize action and thinking, an all-too-common move in the study of ritual. Ritual is a way of thinking and knowing. The point is simply that our ideas and feelings about ritual are shaped not only within ritual itself but also through texts and other media. The Hebrew Bible, for example, includes prescriptive ritual texts, detailing and codifying how to worship and perform sacrifice; that book also contains critical reflection on the social and moral value of those very rites. Confucian texts, in particular the *Book of Rites*, have a great deal to say about the relationship between ritual and social harmony. Travelers' tales, missionary reports, soldiers' journals, scholarly histories—these and other texts variously reveal fascination, disdain, and confusion in regarding the rites of others. Literature and, more recently, film, often includes ritual scenes drawn from daily life. Some literary genres even take on ritual forms: Chaucer's *Canterbury Tales* is a fictionalized pilgrimage, and the literary theorist Mikhail Bakhtin argues that the modern novel came into being through incorporating characteristics of medieval Carnival, a ritual genre that was widely suppressed across Europe in the modern era.

This book introduces a trail of thinking about ritual that is roughly a century old, a broad area of inquiry sometimes referred to as "ritual studies." Ritual studies emerged as a nameable field in the late 1970s and early 1980s, drawing on earlier work in ethology, anthropology, sociology, and the history and phenomenology of religions, and influenced by emerging interdisciplinary interests in such matters as performance, embodiment, authority, power, and creativity. The fundamental questions informing ritual studies are relatively straightforward: What is ritual? What does it do? Is ritual useful? What are the various kinds of ritual? Is ritual tradition bound and conservative, or creative and transformational? Answers to these fundamental questions are diverse and sometimes at odds with each other. The task here is to set down some fence posts that mark out a field of study, in the hopes that the reader will continue to graze.

Chapter 1
Ritualization

The concept of ritualization is one of the cornerstones of ritual studies, though the term has different meanings and uses. The first scholars to systematically develop the notion were ethologists, students of animal behavior, so this is where we will begin our inquiry. Ritual is often associated with religion and therefore with the sacred, with matters heavenly, transcendent, of ultimate importance. It may seem odd then to begin with a discussion of animal behavior and an ethological perspective on ritual. Culturally speaking, there has been a tendency to identify ritual as among those activities and capacities—language, reason, the use of symbols and tools—that distinguishes and separates human beings from other animals. The work in ethology on animal ritualization, however, suggests that ritual is also what connects us to our biological kinfolk.

Seeing ritual

The work of Charles Darwin is representative of a sea change in the kinds of methods employed to study animals. In nineteenth-century Britain, there arose a novel idea: rather than focus on refining systems of classification based on detailed anatomical study of dead animals, it would be better to exchange the morgue-like setting of zoological laboratories and study the behavior of living animals in their natural habitats. The amateur ornithologists who took to the forests and fields of rural Britain at the turn of the twentieth century to patiently observe birds (rather than collect specimens) ushered in new approaches and attitudes in the biological sciences, creating a new kind of job description and specialization—that of the naturalist. The early naturalists laid the groundwork for the emergence of the academic field of *ethology*, the study of animal behavior.

Pursuing close, detailed observations of animals, naturalists and ethologists were struck by certain kinds of behaviors that seemed to them ritual-like in character. In the effort to generate rich descriptions of the bird and animal behaviors they were observing, naturalists had recourse to tropes and language drawn from the world of human culture, especially the domains of ritual, theater, play, and games. The journals, notebooks, and publications of pioneering naturalists such as Edmond Selous, Henry Eliot Howard, and Frederick B. Kirkman make generous use of words such as dance, ceremony, play, posture, attitude, antics, scenes, performances, gesture, and ritual.

The study of ritual from an ethological perspective has built into it a kind of circularity. The detailed study of animal behavior, of their "ceremonies," can tell us something about human ritual, we assume; but it is human ritual that allowed ethologists to perceive animal behavior in ritual terms in the first place. Frederick Kirkman makes this point when he reports how, on one particular day, after several months of observing Black-headed Gulls and Terns, he suddenly was able to see the birds gesturing and posturing.

> In the observations noted during that period I find but one reference to various gestures of these species. Yet the birds must have been posturing daily before my eyes. I had eyes, but not seeing eyes for the particular set of facts...[one day] my eyes were, so to speak, unveiled.

Ritual is not only something that people (and animals) engage in; it is also a way of regarding things. Ritual is both action and idea, and this fact can make it a slippery fish.

On one hand, in order to think critically and analytically about ritual we need to keep these two dimensions (action and idea) distinct. Ritual as a category is not the same thing as ritual enactment, and a great deal of gray matter has been sacrificed on the altar of definitional and conceptual clarity, with some scholars going so far as to claim that the idea or category of ritual is entirely a scholarly construct, loaded with Western assumptions and biases, and not at all descriptive of a real phenomenon. This is not quite my view of the matter, and we will return to the thorny definitional question. On the other hand, the category or idea of ritual shapes the kinds of behaviors and actions we identify as ritual. What, then, did ethologists such as Kirkman suddenly see in the behavior of birds that led them to think and frame their observations in the language of ritual? In short, their attention was drawn to conspicuous behavior, conspicuous by virtue of being patterned, stylized, repetitive, and, surprisingly, communicative.

Honeybees perform an intricate series of abdominal waggles and footwork upon returning to the hive from food gathering. A bee will shuffle around in the shape of a figure eight, while also moving their abdomen up and down. Other bees gather to observe the performance. When we watch bees do this, we may say the bees are "dancing," as the zoologist Max von Frisch did. In 1946, he proposed the idea that these complex and apparently random movements were in fact a means of communication, with the distance and direction to a profitable flower patch signaled by the angle and duration of the waggling. For several decades, the notion was controversial, not the least reason for which is that the power of language had for centuries made communication the provenance of human beings, singular evidence of a distinct ontological difference between human and animal. Sophisticated tests employing radar have indeed confirmed, however, that bees, through movement, are communicating directions to food supplies, just as Frisch had originally argued. Current research further suggests that the waggle dance also communicates information about predation risk. Exactly how this all works is not fully understood, but that the waggle dance is an act of communication is now widely accepted in the scientific community. Ritual, in turn, has been widely theorized as communicative action, with gestures, acts, and utterances a chiefly nonlinguistic means of sending messages—ritual as a form of discourse. This means that ritual, like verbal communication, requires interpretation, and, like the spoken word, is subject to ambiguities, misunderstandings, and deceptions. Moreover, as with linguistic forms of communication, it is not easy to say precisely how ritual works.

The "dance of the bees" is an example of *ritualization*, introduced as a theoretical concept by Julian Huxley in a now famous paper published in 1914 on the courtship habits of the Great Crested Grebe, a species of waterfowl widely distrusted across Europe. In his paper, Huxley distinguishes between *instrumental* and *communicative* behavior. Instrumental behavior favorably modifies an organism's environment, say, in building a nest. Communicative behavior transmits information between the members of a species for their mutual benefit. Huxley's case study of Crested Grebe courtship dealt with a behavioral repertoire in which one partner echoes the movements of the other in a rhythmic, patterned dance. The climax of the ceremony sees the partners, in unison, lifting their bodies out of the water, long, graceful necks reaching to the sky, and rapidly running across the water's surface. Huxley viewed this behavior not only as signaling readiness to mate but also as a means of establishing social bonds and mutually advantageous emotional states.

Huxley argued that these conspicuous patterns of movement and gesture displayed by the Crested Grebe must have, in the course of evolution, lost their original, instrumental function to become purely symbolic ceremonies. Whatever is accomplished physically

1. A pair of Great Crested Grebes posturing during the mating ceremony. The evolutionary biologist Julian Huxley based his theory of ritualization on the observation of such conspicuous, communicative animal behavior.

through movement and posturing, there is an accompanying pattern of meaning and significance to those movements. The relationship between embodiment and meaning is apparent in a phrase such as "body language," or the double meaning of the word "attitude," which refers to both the arrangement and position of a body in space and to a feeling or emotional state.

This process of building up communicative behavior out of originally instrumental acts Huxley termed, with a nod to the

9

world of human ritual, "ritualization." Huxley's image of "courtship" may have made the Crested Grebe seem all too human, but it had the effect of drawing together into the same theoretical orbit the biological and evolutionary processes that give rise to animal ceremonies and the cultural processes that shape human ritual. Some critics see Huxley's argument as a loose analogy, but he was convinced that animal ritual and human ritual had similar functions and purposes.

Ritualization theory

Ritualization theory attempts to explain the presence and development of conspicuous anatomical features and behavioral repertoires in animals. Ethologists ask two key questions: How did these behaviors come to be? What are these behaviors for? In a nutshell, ethology postulates that ritualization is a selective process that allows for the enhanced communication of evolutionary advantageous information and emotional states. In Huxley's words,

> Ritualization may be defined ethologically as the adaptive formalization or canalization of emotionally-motivated behaviour, under the…pressure of natural selection so as (a) to promote better and more unambiguous signal function, both intra- and inter-specifically; (b) to serve as more efficient stimulators or releasers of more efficient patterns of action in other individuals; (c) to reduce intra-specific danger; and (d) to serve as sexual or social bonding mechanisms.

The notion of ritualization in ethology proposes a process through which animal rituals develop. An originally instrumental behavior changes its function to become a communicative behavior. This new behavior becomes independent of its original motivation, and derives from motivations associated with communicating emotional states. These movements become increasingly exaggerated, rhythmic, stylized, and stereotypical, which decreases

the ambiguity of the behavior as a signaling mechanism.
In addition to stylized movements, conspicuous body parts and coloring evolve, which makes the behavior an even more effective means of communication. In ethology, ritualized behavior is functional; it improves communication in potentially troublesome situations associated with mating, feeding, controlling territory, and establishing social hierarchies and bonds.

Ritualization theory is based on conflict models of inner emotional states. Animal ceremonies evolve, so the reasoning goes, in response to having to manage emotional discord created by ambivalence inherent in the conflict created by two or more behavioral tendencies that may lead to trouble. Sexual attraction, for example, draws a pair close together, but proximity also produces fear and the desire to flee, on one hand, and hostility and aggression on the other. A balanced attitude from the extremes of flight or fight is required for successful mating, and the ritualization of appeasing gestures and displays is the route to establishing such attitudes.

Ethologists and biologists understand ritualization as a remarkably flexible evolutionary process, which builds upon convenient behavior patterns and morphological structures in such a way as to enhance communication, create social bonds and hierarchies, appease aggression, establish territory, share food, regulate mating, and reduce intragroup hostilities among individuals. In calling these behavior patterns "ritualizations," ethologists are drawing on certain features of the rites human beings perform—in particular, the stylized, repetitive, performative, and stereotyped nature of many rites and ceremonies.

Human ritualization

In naming specific behavioral patterns of animals "ritualizations" ethologists shaped new attitudes toward the rites we humans perform. The discovery of animal rituals brought human rites and ceremonies, often associated with lofty concerns, back down to earth, linking ritual to everyday run-of-the-mill social life, locating ritual in the body and group interactions rather than in the heavens. The work in ethology contributed to developments in ethnology, the study of human culture and groups, the forerunner of today's cultural anthropology. Ethological and ethnological research at the turn of the twentieth century stimulated the development of the functionalist approaches to thinking about ritual that dominated early sociology and anthropology.

The science of ethology claims that ritualization is part of the biological inheritance of humankind. We like to think of ourselves as free, autonomous agents, so the idea of ritualization, which has an element of universality and determinism to it, perhaps strikes us as limiting. Without question, adaptability, creativity, and choice are distinct human capacities. But ethology asks us to consider that there are also biological action and reaction patterns that govern our behavior, especially in the area of social life. The ethologist Irenäus Eibl-Eibesfeldt has compiled a vast array of such behaviors having to do with stimulus-response mechanisms in newborns, facial expressions, appeasing gestures, sexual identity and pair formation, and the socialization of aggressive behavior. Eibl-Ebesfeldt laid bare a universal grammar of expression and behavior that works alongside—sometimes independently, sometimes in conjunction with—culturally learned behaviors. There is universality, for example, in the human smile, an observation first developed by Darwin. Of course, such claims are debated, partly because the general tenor of postmodern thought derides essences and universal claims, and partly because of the obvious role played by culture in shaping our behavior, beliefs, and values.

Human behavior is the least instinctually determined of all animals. We make our way in the world not merely on the basis of our biological endowment but through the range of signifying practices that constitute culture. In some societies, ritual plays a greater cultural role than in others. For some theorists of ritual, rites and ceremonies are the primary vehicle for the creation of extrinsic behavioral templates, necessary supplements to our genetic inheritance. There is a temporal dimension to the argument proposed by many ethologists and cultural anthropologists. Ritualization theory is grounded in an evolutionary perspective; it tells us that ritual is older than humanity, a notion contrary to intellectualist traditions of thought, which see ritual as the expression of antecedent ideas or beliefs. If ideation, the capacity to hold beliefs, and moral discrimination are unique markers of humanity, perhaps these very powers are derivative of ritual, not the origin of it. Such is the claim of anthropologist Roy Rappaport, whose thesis is embedded directly in the title of his magnum opus, *Ritual and Religion in the Making of Humanity.* A further argument advanced by some proponents of ritualization theory is that the modern West has undervalued the central importance of ritual to social life; in so doing, modernity has turned away from an innate, embodied intelligence and know-how.

Let us consider a specific case of ritualization in human cultures. Many species employ intraspecific aggression in the form of contests to control territory, establish social hierarchies, and regulate mating. Such contests may be tournaments, where physical competition takes place, or displays, behavior that involves no physical contact but rather a show of prowess and determination. A typical tournament scene is that of two deer interlocking antlers and engaging in a test of strength, a different repertoire of behavior than defending an attack by a mountain lion. Inter- and intraspecific aggression are different; the latter is generally understood as adaptive ritualized behavior that prevents serious injury through the use of stereotyped postures, repetitive, stylized movements, and vocalizations. Cats, for example, do not display hunting behavior when they fight with each other; rather, expressive threat postures, screeching calls, and attack with claws (not the teeth, which are used to kill prey), are sufficient to drive away an opponent. Although such contests can leave combatants injured, generally one withdraws before serious injury; death is uncommon.

In contests of display, there is very little or no physical contact whatsoever. The winner is the one who carries on for the longest; the loser is the contestant that gives up interest in continuing. In the case of the mountain gorilla, threat behavior has evolved into the bluff attack. The mountain gorilla performs a bluff attack accompanied by vocalizations, chest thumping, the stomping of feet, and the tearing out and throwing of foliage. Bluff attack is even used in contact with intruders and is usually sufficient to deal with the potential threat.

"Why," asks the sociobiologist E. O. Wilson, "do animals prefer pacifism and bluff to escalated fighting?" The answer seems to be that aggressive behavior is potentially advantageous in marking out territory and ensuring the transmission of one's genetic material, but also potentially harmful to the individual. There are benefits and costs to aggressive competition for food, sexual partners, and territory. A conflict situation can be dealt with through retreat or challenge. In natural environments, asymmetrical contests are typical. Stronger opponents are likely to charge and win, weaker opponents likely to quickly retreat to avoid injury.

Bluffing and agonistic contests are the means through which opponents are able to test their relative strengths, sizing up the situation, as it were, so as to avoid the potential losses associated with actual conflict. Ritualized fighting, in other words, is less harmful than actual fighting. As an evolutionary strategy, possessing nonlethal behavioral repertoires to settle disputes with conspecifics is in the best interests of a species. If this is true of animals, is it true of the human animal, too?

Ethologists argue that ritualized adaptations play a role in human aggression. Diverse cultures practice contests of display, as well as tournaments and duels, both with and without weapons. Traditional Inuit culture employs drumming matches and singing duels to deal with conflict situations. Someone who believes himself wronged by insult, theft, or injury may challenge his opponent to a singing duel, which takes place publicly, in the enclosed confines of the igloo. Jokes, insults, and derision, delivered with a sarcastic and mocking tone, are staples of the match, accompanied by dramatic enactments, such as pretending to sew the opponent's mouth shut, sticking out one's buttocks, or breathing in the face of the opponent. The opponent, for his part, is to take in the performance with reserve and equanimity, until his turn comes to sing complaints and insults. In this way, mistakes, misdeeds, faults of character, and perceived wrongs are freely and publically aired, a process that relieves such wrongs of their potency to generate violence. Typically, the contest ends with a reconciling feast. Such duels can last for days, even years, and are conducted both within and across communities.

One of the first anthropologists to theorize these singing duels was E. Adamson Hoebel, writing in 1941:

> As the court-room joust may become a sporting game between sparring attorneys-at-law, so the juridical song contest is above all things a contest in which pleasurable delight is richly served, so richly that the dispute-settlement function is nearly forgotten. And in the forgetting the original end is the better served. In these ways, Eskimo society, without government, courts, constables, or written law, maintains its social equilibrium, channeling human behavior according to its own accepted standards, buttressing the control dikes along the channels with primitive legal mechanisms, or their equivalents.

Hoebel's study is mired in a colonial perspective of primitivism, a widespread problem in many early studies of ritual; what it shows, however, is that traditional Inuit placed a high value on the public resolution of disputes through a variety of juridical forms, from wrestling to head-butting to song duels. Unlike juridical systems premised on the administration of justice and the meting out of punishment, traditional Inuit practices emphasized conflict resolution and the restoration of the peace through ritualized contests.

The ritualization of conflict situations and aggression through contests and duels is generally understood as a social control mechanism. Max Gluckman, in the context of his ethnographic work in Africa, referred to such practices as "rites of rebellion," enactments that allow conflict to be staged and acted out. Such expressive behavior mitigates, argues Gluckman, against the escalation of aggression and violence by allowing it to be safely expressed and released, thereby serving the maintenance of social order. The ritualization of aggression puts the brakes on runaway aggression that can lead to a destructive escalation of innate aggressive tendencies.

Warfare

A significant step-up in violence from contests and duels is warfare. There is some evidence that war, by which we mean organized, collective, and destructive intergroup violence, is part of the biological record. Jane Goodall shocked the scientific community with her reports of warlike patterns of behavior among a chimpanzee population, which even included episodes of cannibalism. What is perhaps most surprising about war, however, is not that a few other species seem to practice it but that so few do. War is conspicuous partly because of its relative absence among our animal kin. Although the practice of war draws on innate dispositions, war is principally a social or cultural institution, a human-all-too-human affair; as such, it can be prevented.

For war to take place, biological inhibitions against killing, articulated through ritualizations, need to be overcome so that combatants no longer respond to these ritualized signals of submission, appeasement, bonding, and sympathy. During the First World War, there were incidents of sharing food and conversation across trench-lines, acts that made killing all the more difficult; for this reason, troops were regularly rotated so that bonds of sympathy could not be developed. Further, the enemy must be "dehumanized," a process that places the enemy outside one's group, making them a different species, thus eliminating biological inhibitions against killing conspecifics. Ritual and the ritualization of behavior can be used for a variety of purposes. Ritual plays a part in producing soldiers who are immune to signals of appeasement and sympathy, and therefore create an enemy shorn of a human face. The phrase "beating the drums of war" refers to the ritualized production of a populace in favor of war, through the use of parades, mass gatherings, speeches, songs, and hymns. The use of torture in the War on Terror is an example of how the ritualization of violence and cruelty dehumanizes and creates the enemy through the performance of power. Ritualized violence is intentional bodily harm that has been encoded with meanings and used as a tool to communicate values, narratives, and beliefs. The pain experienced by victims of torture is all too real, yet also a kind of performance staged for communicative effect. On the other hand, there exist behavioral repertories, enhanced and developed through cultural rites, which work against the escalation of killing during warfare.

One of the significant facts of human warfare in so-called primitive cultures is its highly ritualized character. Early twentieth-century anthropological studies of indigenous peoples abound with descriptions and generally praiseworthy claims about the civility of their warfare. Roy Rappaport's *Pigs for the Ancestors* (1968) is a study of the ritual and ceremonial life of Tsembaga people of the western highlands of Papua New Guinea.

Traditionally, the Tsembaga are pig herders, and a centerpiece of their ritual life is holding cyclical festivals in response to ecological dynamics associated with the pig population; when the pig population grows too large and threatens the yam crops, a festival is called to cull the herd. The festival period is also a declared time for engaging in warfare, the principal aim of which is to deal with grievances and conflicts that have built up in the time between festivals, and to appease the spirits of ancestors. Rappaport distinguishes between minor and major episodes of war making. Minor war among the Tsembaga, though potentially deadly, is so highly stylized—the arrows used are not even fletched—that casualties are rare.

Typically, warfare as practiced among indigenous peoples on the periphery of industrial society is said to be highly ritualized and, as a result, relatively harmless when compared with modern warfare of industrial civilization. Though there is debate about the claim, this anthropological view of the inherent sensibility of "primitive" warfare has filtered into more popular ideas. The historian of war Gwynne Dyer claims that hunting-gathering societies understand and practice war as "an important ritual, an exciting and dangerous game, and perhaps even as an opportunity for self-expression, but it is not about power in any modern sense of the word, and it is most certainly not about slaughter." Modern warfare, so this line of argument contends, is waged with violence and costs far beyond that of primitive warfare due not only to technological advances in weaponry but due to a de-ritualization of the practice of war. Tom Driver has suggested that the loss of ritualized pathways in the conduct of war is partly responsible for the phenomenon of "total war," war waged with no regard for limits or constraints:

> [W]ithout the channeling and moderation that ritualization
> provides, all contact between living things easily turns into combat
> without limit. If ritualization has provided the evolutionary
> pathways along which we have passed into the human condition, it

18

also provides those that are necessary to keep us there.... Where warfare is ritualized, the combatants do everything possible to make themselves visible to one another. They display themselves vauntingly. They conduct the battle as much by self-advertisement as by their techniques of killing. The flamboyant costume of New Guinea fighters is ingredient to their military skill.... Warfare in the twentieth century turns its back on all this.

Driver's is a bold claim. The premise, however, is worth considering: cultural factors can override "evolutionary pathways," creating behavior that is maladaptive to human flourishing. As ritualization is a component in the selection process of evolution, we would do well to acknowledge in our cultural forms and practices a basic, embodied intelligence in ritualized behavior.

Merits and limits

Of course, you may be thinking that there is a big difference between dancing bees and dancing people, and you would be right. In dance we can improvise, whereas bees are behaving (and can only behave) in accordance with genetic codes. The bees cannot make a mistake nor can they be disingenuous; they cannot lie; they cannot dance ironically; they cannot dance with extra passion; they cannot, presumably, become bored while dancing. What then is gained through a biological approach to ritual? What does ethology contribute to our understanding of human ritual, and what are its limitations?

A serious shortcoming of the ethological notion of ritualization is that the net it casts reaches too far. Simple-celled organisms, for example, can be said to exhibit ritualized behavior. But is it actually helpful to consider the amoeba, whose behavior is invariant, repetitive, and stereotyped, in the same conceptual class as a congregation singing a hymn Sunday morning? Likely not. And yet, there are similarities between certain features of human and animal ritual, features such as repetition, patterning, and stylization. Furthermore, some human rites have functional ends similar to those found in animal ritualization—forming social bonds, for example. Is talk of animal "ceremonies" based on substantive connections between animal behavior and human ritual action, or is it a strained analogy? The debate around this question continues, but the notion of ritualization has widespread currency in ethology, cultural anthropology, psychology, and the cognitive sciences.

Finding similarities, formal or functional, between human and animal ceremonies is perhaps more heuristically useful than proof of evolutionary propositions. Certainly not all human rites lead back in lockstep to animal ritualizations. To trace the beginnings of present day rites and ceremonies across millions of years of evolutionary history seems overly optimistic. At times, the ethological approach can seem overly reductive and explanatory, equating, for example, a priest pouring libations to an animal marking its territory with bodily fluids.

An ethological perspective on ritual, however, places limits on "culturalism," the tendency to frame and explain all human behavior as the product of relatively arbitrary cultural forms. The ethology of ritual demonstrates that we are the product of both nature and culture. Ritual is a window through which one can peer in two directions—toward our biological or animal being and our cultural being; it is also the point at which these dimensions intersect, mingle, and influence one another. Morality is commonly yoked to reflection, the weighing of options, and rational decision making; ethology suggests that there is an innate, bodily intelligence at work in ritualized behavior, an intelligence that we ignore at our peril. In the case of warfare, the culturally constructed norm that makes killing a virtuous duty overrides the biologically formed ritualized behavior that dulls the edge of destructive violence in service of survival.

Ritual

Chapter 2
Ritual and the origins
of culture

One of the implications of the ethological perspective is that ritual must have been present at the very beginnings of humanity. Some early and influential ritual theory presumed that rites and ceremonies emerged in human societies as an articulation and expression of ideas and myths; ethology tells a different story. It is not as though we evolved as human beings and then at some point decided to start doing ritual; rather, ritualization played an adaptive role in the course of both biological and cultural evolution. Look as far back in time as we can—through the textual, archeological, and biological records—and ritual is present. For this reason, speculations about the beginnings of human culture has persistently focused on the contribution and role of ritual.

Werner Herzog's Academy Award-winning film *Cave of Forgotten Dreams* (2010) is a stunning presentation of the wonder of the Chauvet caves. Located in southern France, the network of caves was discovered in 1994. Geologically, the caves are fascinating because of their pristine state and unusually large size and extent. The claim to fame of Chauvet and other such caves is that they contain treasures—exquisite and evocative collections of the world's earliest known art. Dating back some 30,000 years to the Upper Paleolithic era, the undulating and textured walls of Chauvet bring to life the predatory world of lions, panthers, horses, rhinos, bears, and owls. Along with torched-scorched walls, the charred remains of fires, handprints, and the tracks and skulls of bears, the caves at Chauvet delicately preserve the world's earliest known footprint—that of a young child, tantalizingly situated next to the paw print of a wolf. "Did a hungry wolf stalk the boy?" asks Herzog in his narration. "Or did they walk together as friends? Or were their tracks made thousands of years apart? We'll never know."

The rhythm of the film is shaped by a series of descents and ascents, with each return to the surface contextualizing the emotional power of the images with scientific and aesthetic interpretations and speculations about the Paleolithic worldview. In the climax of this rhythmic movement, we return one last time to the cave. We have just heard, above ground, from the French archaeologist Jean Clottes, who led the initial research on the caves and is an advocate of shamanistic interpretations of the culture that produced the art at Chauvet. The art in the caves, Clottes tells us, suggests that *Homo spiritualis*, "spiritual man," is a far better description of our deep nature than is *Homo sapiens*, "the one who knows." Cutting immediately back to the recesses of the cave, the camera focuses on a bear skull suggestively resting at the edge of a large, flat rock, about three feet off the ground. "The strongest hint of something spiritual, some religious ceremony in the cave, is this bear skull," narrates Herzog. "It has been placed dead center on a rock resembling an altar. The staging seems deliberate. The skull faces the entrance of the cave, and around it fragments of charcoal were found, potentially used as incense. What exactly took place here only the paintings could tell us." Has Herzog presented to us traces of a primal ritual scene? Skull, altar, incense, evocative art, shadows and light—the cave seems like a ritual site, or so we are moved to imagine.

Though ritual is something we do, it is often the subject of our imaginative lives, taken up in art, music, literature, and film; in

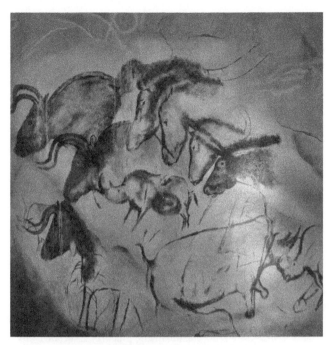

2. **The prehistoric art of the Chauvet caves in southern France concentrates on representations of horses and bison—animals central to Paleolithic hunting culture. Some theorists suggest this cave art originated in the visionary experiences of participants in prehistoric rituals.**

the effort to understand human origins, the imagination of ritual takes center stage, as Herzog demonstrates in his beautifully allusive film.

Shamanic rites

From an anatomical perspective, humans, *Homo sapiens sapiens*, emerged some 200,000 years ago, in the Middle Paleolithic period. From a behavioral perspective, however, many scientists point to the Upper Paleolithic (36,000–10,000 YBP), as the moment in time when characteristics and capacities recognized as distinctly human exploded on the scene, the so-called Great Leap Forward. Herzog's film is informed by this notion of a Paleolithic cultural revolution, directing our attention to the existence of a number of defining universals that constitute human beings in the world: language, symbolism, abstraction, food preparation, artistic expression, music, games, burial, and the use of tools.

Initial efforts at interpreting the significance of Paleolithic cave art advanced an "art for art's sake" view; cave art was understood to be chiefly decorative and expressive. But following on the heels of Mircea Eliade's influential book *Shamanism: Archaic Techniques of Ecstasy* (1951), which identified shamanism's chief characteristic as ritually induced or mediated ecstatic states of consciousness, Paleolithic cave art came to be linked to religious and magical practices associated with shamanistic trance.

The word "shamanism" comes from the Tungus people of Siberia and was employed by late-nineteenth-century missionaries and ethnographers who used it to describe a ritual genre subsequently discovered across circumpolar cultures, practices associated with hunting, healing, the ferrying of the dead to the otherworld, and an animistic sense of an ensouled world of spirits or powers. Many anthropologists working in the late nineteenth and early twentieth centuries understood these shamanistic traditions as the descendants of an original, Paleolithic shamanism. The archaeologist J. D. Lewis-Williams sums up the argument for shamanic interpretations of Paleolithic cave art:

> [T]he antiquity and ubiquity of altered states of consciousness, the widespread occurrence of shamanism among hunter-gatherers, and formal parallels between elements of the mental imagery of altered states and Upper Paleolithic parietal imagery are three points that suggest that at least some—not necessarily all—parietal art was probably associated with institutionalized hallucinations. In other words, it seems highly probable that some yet to be precisely

defined forms of shamanism were present at, probably, all periods of the Upper Paleolithic of western Europe.

If the Paleolithic era was a "great leap" in cultural forms and cognitive capacities, the point where humans fully arrived on the scene, and if cave art is best understood as the product of shamanic practices, then shamanism becomes the original religious or spiritual expression of humanity, and the caves a kind of womb, the moment and place where such fecund ritualized acts were conceived. To this school of thought, cave art signifies a tremendous advance in representational skills. With these skills comes a corresponding cognitive development, the ability to enter altered states of consciousness and then fix the visions experienced in aesthetic forms. These experiences and their representation in art give rise to conceptions of alternative or parallel, frequently tiered, realities. Ritual then is the means and medium for generating and interpreting such experiences.

If we imagine such a ritual scene, deep in the recesses of the Chauvet caves, what would we see? Small numbers of our Paleolithic ancestors descend into the dangerous territory of the caves. Perhaps a charismatic individual leads them, revealing and inducting new members into the mysteries of the underworld. There, in the shadows and light cast by torches, they drum, sing, and reach out to the textured surface of the walls, with their cracks, folds, and hidden recesses. The skulls and bones of animals are handled and enshrined in niches or on rocks, which serve as our earliest altars. Images of animals are painted; earlier paintings are revered as icons of the intimate relation between human and animal worlds, and as links to the group's ancestors. The impulse to leave the daily world of light and safety for the dangers of the caves suggest an urge to seek out a distinct place for extraordinary acts, a place that by virtue of its very separation from ordinary life was perhaps thought to offer knowledge and experience of the world in its totality.

Functionally, such shamanic rites may have well served the needs of early hunting societies. The challenges and problems associated with securing food, the most basic of life's necessities, could be worked through in ritual form. By symbolically enacting the hunt, our Paleolithic ancestors may have gained some measure of control and power over a precarious and demanding part of daily life. Walter Burkert suggests that "men penetrated into those dark caves; and as they repeated this symbolic quest [for food], it became an established ritual: to penetrate, by a daring and difficult exploit, into those underground chambers in order to reestablish and bring back the hope of affluence." Burkert further speculates that out of this ritual "questing" grew the myths and epics that would form the basis of the earliest literature of the ancient Near East and Greece—heroic tales of exploits, questing, and seeking.

We often find in ritual enactment references and resemblances to daily practices. Burkert tacitly invokes a conception of ritual developed by the historian of religion Jonathan Z. Smith. For Smith, "ritual is a means of performing the way things ought to be in conscious tension to the way things are in such a way that the ritualized perfection is recollected in the ordinary, uncontrolled course of things." The expression of a tension or discrepancy between the haphazardness of daily life and the formalized, repetitive, idealized perfection of ritual is, for Smith, ritual's principal function. Ritual is a performance of the ideal, in full relationship with the messiness of life. For Smith, ritual is a special cultural space where life can be imagined, staged, watched, practiced, done right, and then, hopefully, recollected in daily life—but always with the understanding of a gap or distance between ritual and ordinary life. Ritual is in part a model for action, but even more profoundly ritual discloses and enacts the experience of distance and tension between what is and what is hoped for, between the real and the unattainable, actuality and possibility.

Ritual architecture

As we move from the Paleolithic to the Neolithic era, roughly 10,000–3500 BCE, we have more archaeological data on which to base theories of ritual in early communities. If cave art exemplifies the achievements of Paleolithic culture, a defining feature of the Neolithic period is the widespread appearance of large-scale building projects. The site of Göbekli Tepe in southern Turkey is one of earliest known examples of megalithic architecture, built some 11,000 years ago, an astonishing seven millennia before the Great Pyramid of Giza. The site is located in a remote, mountainous region, some distance from the settlement of Urfa. People did not live at Göbekli Tepe, and it was not a burial site. Rather, people traveled several miles to work on it and visit.

The cleanly carved reliefs on the large limestone blocks and pillars (the tallest are eighteen feet high and weigh sixteen tons) include anthropomorphic forms, geometric shapes, and a variety of animals: snakes, scorpions, spiders, gazelles, foxes, ducks, and crocodiles. The pillars are arranged in nested, concentric rings, forming a series of enclosures, interconnected with walls and benches; the size of the enclosures vary, holding anywhere from a few dozen to a hundred people. More than two hundred pillars have been unearthed, and those nearer the center of the structure are larger, more finely hewn, and covered with detailed, carved bas-reliefs.

Klaus Schmidt, one of the lead investigators at the site, refers to Göbekli Tepe as the world's "first temple" and a "religious sanctuary." Many archaeologists to have investigated the site agree that its principal use was as a religious and ritual center, rather than a settlement, and this fact is placing received narratives about the development of Neolithic culture into question. The standard tale of cultural evolution tells of an agriculturally based transition from small-scale, nomadic, hunter-gathering groups to larger, settled communities. With the rise of agriculture and permanent settlements, new forms of social organization are called for, promoting cooperation, establishing the divisions of labor, and maintaining social statuses and hierarchies characteristic of large-scale communal life: Enter religion and ritual. The evidence at Göbekli Tepe complicates this narrative, argues Schmidt, who suggests that the site itself may have been fundamental in the shift to agriculture and the practice of congregating in larger communities. In Schmidt's interpretation, groups of foragers living in a radius around Göbekli Tepe came together to build a massive temple complex, which in turn stimulated the rise of more permanent, agriculturally based settlements.

> The function of these buildings can only be characterized as associated with ritual purposes, and no serious claim for domestic use is tenable. It is clear that Gobekli Tepe was not an early Neolithic settlement with some ritual buildings, but that the whole site served a mainly ritual function. It was a mountain sanctuary.

In other words, the building, art, and ritual activity at the site were not instruments to serve social organization—the standard sociological view of ritual's origins and functions—but rather the outcome of ontological interests and ideas out of which emerged the earliest forms of organized, religion. Schmidt imagines scenes of communal feasting, drumming, singing, dancing, the creation of a symbolic sensibility, and a more complex ontology describing the relation between the material and spiritual worlds. Göbekli Tepe emerges in Schmidt's interpretation as an early cultic site, a forerunner of temple sites such as those found at Delphi and Olympia, attracting pilgrims from the surrounding catch basin.

Interpretation of the evidence at sites such as Göbekli Tepe raises questions about the relation between ritual and place. We bring our own cultural presuppositions to the table in interpreting data from the past, and one of the more common ideas, in both scholarly and popular thought, has been the separation of the sacred and the profane as distinct cultural domains, likely a uniquely modern idea. Schmidt's perspective is implicitly premised on Emile Durkheim, who introduced the sacred/profane dichotomy as a foundation for understanding religious phenomena. One assumption often made of ritual is its separateness from ordinary life, hence the need for a special location. In archaeological theory, the early Neolithic temple or shrine becomes ritual's home, a place for ritual "to take place," a phrase coined by Jonathan Z. Smith, who develops the notion that ritual is principally a matter of emplacement.

In Smith's ritual theory, action becomes ritual by virtue of its location. Here, Smith introduces a dichotomy into his theory: ritual, since not ordinary, takes place in nonordinary locales. For Smith, the temple rites of prehistory and antiquity are exemplary of ritual. Ritual, it is thought, happens when, at symbolically significant times and in special places, a group of congregants gather to perform or enact a formal set of acts. The idea, however, that ritual is to be clearly distinguished from ordinary, domestic behavior, as well as necessarily connected with the supernatural or religious, is very much part of modern, Western rationality. Ronald Grimes has critiqued Smith's spatialized theory of ritual, offering several objections to Smith's "reduction of a multidimensional phenomenon [ritual] to a single, key dimension that presumably explains the whole." Grimes favors a more comprehensive analysis of ritual's many components, while emphasizing ritual as a special kind of action, rather than the result of special emplacement.

Dualistic kinds of separations—nature/culture, sacred/profane, living/dead—are characteristic of the Western intellectual tradition, and ethnography has taught us that such distinctions are not easily applied to indigenous cultures, where ritual permeates society. In keeping with ethnographic research, archaeologists such as Richard Bradley, in a manner similar to Grimes, suggests that prehistoric European and Near Eastern sites as easily call into question as support distinctions between quotidian (nonritual) and sacred (ritual) activities.

How does one go about identifying an archaeological site as a sacred site (that is, a site for ritual) in the first place? Generally, it has to be separated from domestic use, contains artifacts such as statuary of gods and goddesses (again, special and distinct from everyday objects), and the sites themselves should be unique (ornate, complex, large beyond need, highly aestheticized, in special locations) when compared with dwelling sites. Here, we detect, Bradley points out, scholarship importing dualistic conceptions of ritual from the modern West back to Neolithic period. Bradley masterfully demonstrates how the contemporary experience of an increasingly secular world, where religion and ritual have been marginalized to take place in a special setting, has led archaeologists to overlook the intimate relationships between ritual and daily, domestic life in prehistoric societies.

Myth and ritual school

Around the turn of the twentieth century there appeared a number of influential studies exploring the relations between myth and ritual in the cultures of the ancient Near East and Mediterranean. In the late Bronze and Iron Ages there emerges a new kind of data in the effort to understand the nature and functions of ritual in early societies—the written text. The work of James Frazer, author of the influential *The Golden Bough: A Study in Magic and Religion*, published in twelve volumes between 1906 and 1915, incorporated comparative textual study of ancient literature, myth, and sacred texts with emerging ethnographies and archeological discoveries. Frazer's work, along with that of Robertson Smith and the generation of scholars that followed them, is broadly referred to as the "myth and ritual school." These scholars shared a basic sense that myth and ritual were closely related, though there was often disagreement on the details, as well as a persistent interest in understanding the relationships between ritual and theatre.

Frazer's *Golden Bough* was particularly influential. His key idea and claim is that underlying all ritual (and myth) is a universal pattern or structure: the death and rebirth of a god or divine king that ensures the fertility of the land as well as social order and harmony. Frazer writes: "the ceremony of the death and resurrection of Adonis must have been a dramatic representation of the decay and revival of plant life." There are many gods of vegetation, like Adonis, central to the mystery cults of ancient Greece. In addition to the myths of Adonis and Osiris, Frazer focused on Dionysus, whose "sufferings, death, and resurrection were enacted in his sacred rites." The premise is that behind these myths and stories recorded in the texts of antiquity is sacrificial ritual. In drawing together the motif of seasonal renewal with myths of sacrificial rites involving death and rebirth, Frazer suggested three things about ritual. First, the original and primary ritual form is that of blood sacrifice. Second, ritual represents natural process or mythic-historical events or narratives. Third, ritual is inherently an act of magic, informed by the idea that "you can produce any desired effect by merely imitating it."

In describing ritual as "dramatic enactment," Frazer set the stage for the so-called Cambridge Ritualists, the classicists Gilbert Murray, Francis Conford, and Jane Harrison. Working chiefly with classical texts, the Cambridge School proposed the theory that theater emerged from ritual. What this meant is that the traces of our earliest rites were preserved, if somewhat hidden and transformed, in classical texts. The formal choral dithyramb of Athenian Dionysian festivals, a hymn sung and danced in competition by groups of up to fifty men and boys, was said to have originated in Dionysian cultic rites. The literary and theatrical genre of tragedy in turn, was said to have emerged from the tradition of the dithyramb. For Harrison, the ritual-theater

31

distinction rests on the transition from a participating congregation to an observing, more detached audience.

The theories proposed by Frazer and the Cambridge School have been largely discredited. Most scholars hold that the evidence does not support the claims made. Before offering some critical reflection, let us consider sacrificial rites, since sacrifice plays such a prominent role in the myth-ritual school; moreover, an interest in sacrifice has been revived in recent decades, through the work of the literary critic René Girard.

Sacrifice

The practice and institution of sacrifice was pervasive in the ancient societies of the Near East, India, and Mediterranean. In 303 CE, the Roman emperor Diocletian, on the occasion of twenty years of rule, erected a monument in Rome. The rectangular bases that supported massive columns were covered in scenes of victory and sacrifice, the emperor in all his glory, at a smoking altar, flanked by various deities and surrounded by the animals and entourage required for the rite known as *Suovetaurilia*. The name derives from the animals sacrificed: a pig (*sus*), sheep (*ovis*), and bull (*taurus*). *Suovetaurilia* was employed on various occasions: to mark an official census, to celebrate military victories, to commemorate jubilees, to atone for ritual errors or transgressions, and in the context of agricultural festivals.

Roman descriptions of agricultural rites tell of families purifying themselves by abstaining from sex, carefully washing, dressing in white, and adorning themselves with wreaths, before circumambulating, three times, the perimeter of fields, animals in tow. Prayers were recited before the animals were slaughtered. The entrails were examined for omens; imperfections would necessitate another animal to be sacrificed, repeatedly, until the perfect specimen was found. Entrails and bones were wrapped in fat and burned on an altar;

3. This section from a Roman altar relief depicts a sacrificial procession. Women, playing a lyre and flute, and soldiers stand by as a priest, accompanied by attendants, pours a libation in preparation for the sacrifice of a bull. Sacrificial rites were the mainstay of pagan religious and civic life in the pre-Christian Mediterranean.

the edible portions would be enjoyed at a banquet. The intentions here seem to have been assuring a bountiful harvest, magically protecting fields through the act of encircling, and appeasing or currying the favor of gods and powers through the offering of choice animals. We can also imagine that such feasts were the occasion for a festive atmosphere and sociability. The mood of similar rites conducted for civic and political purposes were likely more austere and solemn.

Sacrificial traditions were as certainly as old to the era of Diocletian as Diocletian is to us. Visual culture has left a plentiful record of sacrificial rites, and the practice abounds in our oldest texts and literature. One can scarcely turn a page of Homer's *Iliad* without reading of sacrifice:

> At once the men arranged to sacrifice for Apollo,
> Making the cattle ring his well-built altar,
> Then they rinsed their hands and took up barley.
> Rising among them Chryses stretched his arms to the sky
> And prayed in a high resounding voice, "Hear me, Apollo!
> God of the silver bow who strides the walls of Chryse...."
> And soon as the men had prayed and flung the barley,

First they lifted back the heads of the victims,
Slit their throats, skinned them and carved away
The meat from the thighbones and wrapped them in fat....
The work done, the feast laid out, they ate well
And no man's hunger lacked a share of banquet....
And all day long
They appeased the god with song, raising a ringing hymn
to the distant archer god who drives away the plague,
those young Achaean warriors singing out his power,
And Apollo listened, his great heart warmed with joy. (1.534–566)

Homeric sacrifice is generally yoked to the desire to appease the
gods, but also to a communal, convivial spirit. Appeasing the
destructive violence of war, averting plagues and misfortune, is
achieved through the sharing of food and spirits, returning the
combatants to a gentler, sociable mood.

One of the more influential theories of sacrifice has been
developed by the literary critic René Girard. For Girard, violence
is not simply the expression of an instinct or the outcome of
innate aggression; neither is it mainly the result of territoriality
and competition for resources. Rather, violence is the outcome
of what Girard calls imitative desire. For Girard, we are
creatures of imitation, and we imitate not only the behavior of
people but their desires as well. Desiring what someone else
desires causes social conflict. When Thomas Hobbes refers
to the "state of nature" as the "war of all against all," he is
recognizing the way in which conflict can quickly escalate into
a chaotic frenzy.

Unlike social contract theorists such as Hobbes, Girard scoffs at
the idea that in the midst of a contagion of violence, cooler heads
can prevail and, through acts of rationality and willfulness, people
institute limits and constraints on social violence. Searching the
anthropological and textual records, Girard finds evidence for
what he terms the "single victim mechanism," the spontaneous,

accidental, and unconscious discovery that when everyone channels his violence toward a single individual—a victim—social order and harmony is created. Many origin myths point to a founding murder as the origin of culture, such as in the story of Cain and Abel. Culture, says Girard, is founded on a collective murder. Culture begins when people's desire for blood, in the midst of pervasive collective violence, spontaneously unite against a single victim: the war of each against each becomes the unity of all against one—the principle of the scapegoat. And out of the corpse of the scapegoat victim is the sacrificial cult that is the basis of all human culture.

Girard emphasizes that early societies did not really understand what they were doing. The awe-inspiring transmutation of violence into order was so powerful that it generated the notion and experience of the sacred, as sacrificial victims became gods. This error was a necessary illusion, says Girard, because these societies had no other way of maintaining order, and because sacrifice works only when it is believed to be a divine and not a human requirement. The origin of religion and its persistence depends on suppressing, concealing, displacing any evidence of its own violent origins. Sacrifice creates a categorical distinction between sacred and ordinary violence: sacred violence, or sacrifice, is "good" violence. If this distinction collapses, the power of sacrifice to maintain order collapses, and other institutions, such as laws and a judicial system, will be required. Girard refers to the broad societal questioning of the distinction between "good" and "bad" violence as a "sacrificial crisis," a famous example of which is found in the Hebrew prophets, who roundly critiqued the intuition of temple sacrifice, calling for it to be replaced by mercy, justice, and peace.

Scholarly theories, scholarly fantasies

The world's mythic traditions abound with stories of human origins. Questions about the birth of human culture are the stuff of social science no less than myth. Scholarly interest in the origins of our species and the foundations of culture and social institutions such as law, religion, and theater has waxed and waned in the modern period. In the wake of Darwin and evolutionary theory, the question of origins was front and center in biology, anthropology, and comparative religion, which later migrated to the edges of scholarship, only in recent years to make a comeback. Whether scholarly ideas about human origins are best understood as theories or fantasies is an open question. What was the role and function of ritual in the earliest period of cultural evolution? The answers are highly speculative: shamanic trance and the emergence of advanced cognitive abilities; the construction of ritual sites as an expression of existential needs and interests, leading to the growth of large-scale, settled society and the separation of the sacred and profane; sacrifice as a necessary mechanism to control violence and with it the birth of the sacred and religious systems—these narratives, as fascinating as they are, need to be taken with a grain or two of salt.

What many scholars in search of origins seem to be seeking is (to their minds) a more rational and scientific explanation of the religion of their day (typically Christianity, with its emphasis on death and resurrection) in terms of its prehistoric origins in fertility and sacrificial cults. This is certainly true of the myth and ritual school, which was also informed by nostalgia for ritual. In late nineteenth and early twentieth century Europe, ritual was in decline and viewed largely as the remnants of a superstitious, less enlightened age; looking to the distant past and finding ritual everywhere reinforced its absence.

Girard's theory of sacrifice is fascinating, but, like the myth and ritual school, it is based largely on the study of texts and has an apologetic dimension in which Christianity emerges as the revelation of the essential equation of religion and violence in "primitive" societies. Girard's theory has been advanced and promoted by theologians, literary critics, and philosophers, but anthropologists using ethnographic methods to study societies that maintain sacrificial rites find little evidence in support of Girard. Walter van Beek, for example, has studied sacrifice in Cameroon and Nigeria, and he finds little support for Girardian theories in his data.

> According to René Girard [the] scapegoat function is essential in sacrifice, but actually the ritual violence does not generate consensus...theoreticians such as Girard have made too much of the violent act of killing; as I have argued, a ritual sacrifice—be it at home, ward, or village—is no more violent than any major meal, even much less so than a large feast.... It is not the shock of killing a bull, but the joy in having abundant meat that dominates.

What was the nature and function of ritual for our early ancestors living in the Upper Paleolithic and Neolithic eras? What were their ritual lives like? These are, of course, most difficult questions to answer. Not only must we reach across a vast expanse of time, we have so little data. Unlike bones, ritual—as with music, play, and spoken language—does not fossilize. We can locate skeletal and archeological remains, but the remnants of material culture can take us only so far in reconstructing ritual and performance; gestures, postures, moods, rhythms, intentions—these can only be inferred and imagined. And great care is needed when theorizing ritual on the basis of the written text.

Girard describes "the unity of all rites" in sacrifice: rites of passage, healing and magic, festivals, juridical rites, and Greek tragedy. In Girard's creative reading, these all have their origin in blood sacrifice: "all religious ritual springs from the surrogate victim, and all the great institutions of mankind, both secular and religious, spring from ritual." A bold claim indeed. Theories of the "it-all-comes-down-to" variety are overly ambitious; the search for an Ur-ritual as the wellspring of all cultural institutions is intriguing, but it is often an exercise in scholarly mythmaking.

Chapter 3
Ritual and society

Ritualization has a function or purpose—it increases the likelihood of species survival. This functional approach to thinking about ritual has also been a focus of inquiry in the social sciences, where it is generally assumed that ritual, given both its pervasiveness and generally collective, public nature, must be serving some socially useful end. What does ritual do? The dominant answer that developed in the sociological and anthropological theory in the first half of the twentieth century is clear: ritual, whether secular or sacred, binds groups together, ensuring their harmonious functioning by generating and maintaining orders of meaning, purpose, and value.

Emile Durkheim: solidarity and effervescence

In his enormously influential *The Elementary Forms of Religious Life* (1912), based largely on his study of Australian aboriginal ethnography, Emile Durkheim proposed that religion is the basic "social fact." Durkheim considered the ubiquity of religion as a clear indication of its social utility. His idea is that cosmological order articulated in religious traditions is actually the social order unknowingly projected outward and writ large; because the heavenly world is perceived as the source and model for society, social institutions and the forms and habits of everyday life are thereby lent legitimacy and longevity. Durkheim's further step was to argue that religious ideas, beliefs, and values arise from social practices, in particular from a society's principal rites and ceremonies. It is not simply that ritual confirms and reinforces social order; Durkheim suggested that ritual plays a fundamental role in establishing that very sacred/social order, with its corresponding group membership, social roles, status systems, and hierarchies. In Durkheim's hands, ritual emerged in modern scholarship as forge and glue for creating and binding society, an idea that in various forms pervades the social sciences.

For the Durkhemian tradition, ritual is all about tradition; ritual is an inherently conservative institution that joins people into a collective and encourages them to look to the past for models and guidance. Durkheim emphasized the role of ritual in producing *solidarity*, a term connoting both the weightiness of an oak tree and a harmonious working of an ant colony. Talk of "cohesion," "equilibrium," and "integration" abounds in this school of thought. Far from associating ritual strictly with a staid tradition, however, Durkheim wrote of the power of ritual to produce *effervescence*, a bubbly metaphor suggesting well-being, collective joy, exuberance, and flourishing. Too often, this dimension of Durkheim's thought is overlooked.

> To strengthen emotions that would dissipate if left alone the one thing needful is to bring all those who share them into more intimate and more dynamic relationship. . . . The very act of congregating is an exceptionally powerful stimulant. Once the individuals are gathered together, a sort of electricity is generated from their closeness and quickly launches them to an extraordinary height of exaltation. . . . Probably because a collective emotion cannot be expressed collectively without some order that permits harmony and unison of movement, these gestures and cries tend to fall into rhythm and regularity, and from there into songs and dances.

Durkheim is writing here about the creation of the experience of the sacred through ritual action. Such reflections would later shape Victor Turner's discussion of *communitas*, the experience in ritual of blurring or merging self and other, the production of oneness and integrative harmony.

For Durkheim, the very existence of society is something demanding explanation. Society is solidarity and effervescence, and these are the outcome of ritual enactment. One implication of Durkheim's thought is clear: no ritual, no society.

Durkheim would have agreed with the anthropologist Roy Rappaport, who writes: "Humanity is a species that lives and can only live in terms of meanings it itself must invent." Historically, matters of meaning, purpose, and truth have been the purview of the world's religions. In the modern era there are many substitutive domains serving a similar function: science, art, popular culture, sports, civics, and voluntarism. Culture is a supplement for the human being's lack of instinctual determination, a second skin telling us what to think and how to act. For theorists such as Durkheim, Rappaport, Clifford Geertz, and Peter Berger, religion and its secularized equivalents are systems of symbols providing a kind of blueprint or orienting map without which we are lost, unable to order the diverse sensations received from our environment. We get on with life by gathering information stored not only in our physiological makeup but in the cultural goods that surround us, in the intersubjective space of human signifying practices: maps, clothing, food, sacred objects, music, built environments, conceptions of time, and rites and performances.

Rappaport takes this train of thought a step farther. He argues that ritual is not merely one among many meaningful human activities but is rather the original and primary means of creating systems of meaning that ground and give life to society. In spite of the primacy Durkheim gave to ritual enactment, there was a creeping intellectualism in his thought. When Durkheim writes that rituals are "merely the external envelope concealing mental operations," we can see his privileging of ideas over action. For Rappaport, in contrast, in the course of human evolution gestural communication and ritualized behavior antedates other forms of symbolic communication, as well as language and ideation; ideas are the product of ritual action.

A society's identifiable rites comprise what Rappaport terms *liturgical orders*. Reasoning from the fact of the ubiquity and pervasiveness of religion in human cultures, Rappaport suggests that

> in the absence of what we, in a common sense way, call religion, humanity could not have emerged from its pre- or proto-human condition. It is, therefore, plausible to suppose, although beyond demonstration's possibilities, that religion's origins are, if not one with the origins of humanity, closely connected to them.... [Moreover], religion's major conceptual and experiential constituents, the sacred, the numinous, the occult and the divine, and their integration into the Holy, are the creations of ritual.

Rappaport's argument is detailed and complex. His is a formalistic approach, developing in systematic and logical fashion the implications and consequences (what he calls "entailments") of ritual's formal features. He defines ritual as "the performance of more or less invariant sequences of formal acts and utterances not entirely encoded by the performers." Since the substance or content of ritual varies widely across cultures, ritual's uniqueness lies in the conjunction of these formal properties rather than any particular content. The form of ritual, Rappaport suggests, is itself a metamessage that serves to establish conventions, seal the social contract, formulate ideas, inculcate values, and generate and represent collective frameworks of meaning and purpose.

There are two obvious features of ritual, suggests Rappaport. First, ritual has a formal, invariant structure; people, if they engage in ritual, must necessarily—if tacitly—assent and conform to that structure. Second, there is no ritual if it is not performed. To consider ritual as an alternative, secondary medium for expressing what could otherwise be (perhaps more easily) expressed is to miss what is distinctive about ritual: a rite requires performance.

In the tradition of Durkheim, a group of people become a society through a shared experience of the sacred—that object, idea, or belief that is fundamentally valued. Rappaport argues that the binding of people around a shared sense of the sacred is best and perhaps only achieved through ritual. Rappaport's idea is that through a mutually shared and relatively invariant performance, ritual begets a sense of permanence, consistency, reliability, certainty, sanctity, even truth, a general posture toward and experience of the world that cannot be obtained through other means.

Rappaport's is by far one of the most ritually centered theories of ritual; he makes extravagant claims for ritual's efficacy, even its necessity for social life. It is difficult, however, to imagine one particular kind of human action as fundamentally responsible for so much. Rappaport's theory has further trouble dealing with the empirical fact of ritual change. And finally, his emphasis on social unity and experiences of sanctity seems to overlook another empirical fact, namely, that much ritual is filled with explicit or tacit conflict and used for purposes of power and control.

Ritual, politics, and power

In an essay on the symbolism of power, Clifford Geertz writes of the ritual genre of "royal progresses," which "locate the society's center and affirm its connection with transcendent things by stamping a territory with ritual signs of dominance. When kings journey around the country side, making appearances, attending fetes, conferring honors, exchanging gifts, or defying rivals, they mark it, like some wolf or tiger spreading his scent through his territory, as almost physically part of them."

Royal progresses are but one of a wide range of institutional rites and ceremonies serving the interest of political power. Processions and parades, commemorations and jubilees, enthronements and inaugurations, raising the flag and singing the national anthem, potlatches and papal enclaves: many of these rites are either fundamentally political in nature or have important political dimensions.

Central to civic life and the political and legal authority of Venice's ducal office, an institution that lasted for nearly a millennium until 1797, were cycles of processions. A dozen times or more each year, leading civic officeholders would wind their way through the city streets, carrying objects said to represent the authority given to the doge (duke) by Pope Alexander III in 1197. Often taking place on feast days in the liturgical calendar and ending at St. Mark's Basilica, the processions drew on the potency of ecclesiastical rites and symbols but for instrumentally political ends.

These processions were known throughout Europe for their ability to fuse the lavishness of pomp and wealth with the seriousness of pious devotion. Ducal processions were arranged in linear fashion according to social rank and status, revealing class, age, and sex differentiation. Through the early modern period, the classes comprising a growing urban society were distinguished and classified through public, civic rituals with elaborate, hierarchical structures. Processions represented and reproduced the structural features of sociopolitical order; the notion that ritual models the hierarchies, status systems, and power relations of society is a widespread proposition informing ritual theory.

4. The doge leads a procession through the streets of Venice in this
sixteenth-century engraving by Jost Amman, an artist commissioned
to produce a series of images detailing the ceremony. Processions,
the ceremonial heart of the Republic of Venice, were a means
of displaying and validating political power and authority.

Venetian processions are an example of civic or civil ritual, and such politically oriented rites are pervasive across history and geography. In Europe and North America during the eighteenth and nineteenth centuries, state nationalisms began to take on the socially integrative role once played by traditional forms of religion. Historical narratives (myths), monumental buildings and statuary (sacred places), legendary figures (founders and heroes), charters and constitutions (sacred texts), public ceremonies (rituals), and civil holidays (liturgical cycles) worked in unison to form a collective set of beliefs, values, and identity structures associated with the nation. This new nationally oriented worldview was meant to supplant older confessional models. An individual would no longer be principally a Lutheran, a Calvinist, or a Catholic, for example, but a German, a Frenchman, an Englishman. Such efforts were only partly successful, and confessional and national identities in Europe and the Americas intertwined in complex ways.

One example of civil religion is found in Wittenberg, Germany. Wittenberg was the seat of the German Reformation and the home of Martin Luther. Through the nineteenth and early twentieth centuries the kaisers, as part of building a unified German state, transformed Wittenberg into an iconic ceremonial ground. Monuments were commissioned, museums built, churches renovated, and ceremonies performed. Kaiser Wilhelm II spared no expense in making the 1892 Reformation Day festival something to remember. The highest officials from the Evangelical Church attended, as did members of the German parliament. Wilhelm II personally invited the queens of England and Holland and the kings of Denmark and Sweden. The kaiser made his way in a procession from Wittenberg's train station to the newly restored Castle Church. Taking his throne on a large stage built for the occasion, and positioned with a view to the Thesesenportal, a set of massive bronze doors installed to commemorate Luther's legendary (if fictive) posting of the ninety-five theses, Wilhelm II participated in a key ceremony. The architect of the doors came forward carrying the golden key on a cushion. The kaiser stepped down, and, in front of the doors given to the church by his ancestor Frederick IV, with Germany's and Europe's political, economic, and religious elite looking on, passed the key on to the president of the Evangelical Church, who received it with hyperbolic deference. Religion and politics were ritually fused in a normative symbolic object, enacting and mythologizing the Luther story in the course of nation building.

Eric Hobsbawm and T. O. Ranger, in their Marxist-inspired collection of essays on the "invention of tradition," demonstrate how modern nation-states utilized such ceremonial occasions to "inculcate certain values and norms of behavior by repetition, which automatically implies continuity with the past." Hobsbawm argues that the invented nature of tradition must be hidden, in absolutes or timelessness, in order for that tradition to have authority. Ritual pomp and repetition is one way of inventing new forms of social order, while simultaneously obscuring that very act of invention. In November 2011, the Canadian government orchestrated an elaborate military parade and civil ceremony, which included a warplane fly-over of the parliament buildings in Ottawa, to honor the Canadian military's contributions to the ousting of Muammar Gaddafi from power in Libya, a great military success. The ceremony marked something new in Canadian public life, an effort to transition the imagination of Canada's military from its traditional role of "peacekeeping" to a more robust, active, and interventionist role in global conflicts and civil wars. The Libya celebrations met with much skepticism; Canada has never been keen on flag-waving associated with its military. But ritual can be a powerful tool in swaying public opinion and mobilizing public support.

In spite of postmodern sentiments to the contrary, there is nothing inherently wrong with structure, order, and hierarchy, and hence, nothing inherently wrong with rites and ceremonies—religious, political, or otherwise—that play a part in the exercise of power and authority. People need to be affirmed in their beliefs by enacting them, and ritual is surely a source of collective identity for many, while upholding various dimensions of social order. The effervescence, solidarity, and *communitas* that at times accompany collective rites hold disorder, entropy, and chaos at bay, establishing meaningful and purposeful interactions with others. In the spirit of Marx and critical theory, however, there has been a good deal of justified suspicion about social "structures," and the concomitant role of ritual in supporting them. Ritual may well be a kind of social glue, but what if it is holding together a system of domination, oppression, and exploitation?

The politically useful dimensions of ritual have generally been met with suspicion. Consider this passage written by Max Gluckman in his study *Politics, Law and Ritual in Tribal Societies*:

> Tribal rituals entail dramatization of the moral relations of the group...ritual is effective because it exhibits all the tensions and strife inherent in social life itself. Major loyalties are affirmed through the dramatic representation both of many bonds of unity and of the conflicts that lie in these varied bonds....Ritual cloaks the fundamental disharmonies of social structure by affirming major loyalties to be beyond question.

We detect here a suspiciousness of ritual. Ritual "cloaks" (mystifies) the "disharmonies" (inequalities) inherent in social structures, making them seem inherently natural or supernatural, rather than human inventions. Contra Durkheim, Gluckman conceived ritual not in terms of unity and harmony but as an arena of social tensions embodying both the cooperation and struggle inherent in any social group. Ritual does not so much affirm and unify as enact difference and discord in such a fashion that reduces the likelihood of disruptive conflict.

Pursuing this line of thought, Gluckman identified a class of ritual that he termed *rites of rebellion*. He conducted fieldwork in southeast Africa among the Zulu. He discovered there a set of rites, associated broadly with fertility practices, in which girls and women take openly to the streets, wearing men's clothing and herding cattle, an exclusively male occupation. In stages of these rites they also went naked, cursed men, and sang obscene songs, while the boys and men stayed inside at home, as if they were women. Within the frame of the ritual, women were free to dress down men with acts of humiliation and act out in lewd and provocative manners. Gluckman suggests that such practices need to be interpreted in the context of a society in which women are generally subordinate to men and thus largely excluded from the economic and politic spheres. Gluckman called these "bacchantic" rites, with reference to the aggressive Dionysian women of ancient Greece, and he argued they allow for the airing of grievances and frustrations without seriously threatening the social order. Through ritual, the patriarchal nature of Zulu society is in the end affirmed and done a service, by craftily allowing for a periodic release of tensions built up around gender inequalities. Ritual is conceived by Gluckman as a sleight of hand serving the interests of those really in charge.

There are similar kinds of "rebellious" rites in different cultures. The roots of European Carnival traditions so central to social life in the late Middle Ages and early modern period can be traced back to Roman Saturnalia festivals. Such public celebrations depicted a "world turned upside down." The lowly became high, with masters serving servants, and slaves becoming state officials—for a time. The rowdiness and festive atmosphere of Carnival traditions, coupled with the opportunity to poke fun at the high and mighty, is often understood as a means to suspend or alleviate tensions within stratified social classes and relations, a kind of safety valve to keep the pot from boiling over. In this line of thinking, ritual is a chiefly a mechanism of social control.

Ritual as negotiation

We need not, however, take so jaundiced and suspicious a view of ritual's contributions to society. There are many rites that appear to wrestle with the fact of social tensions and discord in a more open and forward-looking, rather than purely stabilizing, fashion. In recent years, the notion of ritual as form of social "negotiation" has gained currency.

Applied to ritual, the term negotiation draws attention to the debates, reflexivity, and grievances—expressed in a shout, delivered with a glance, carried on a banner—present in diverse rites and cultural performances. In a narrower sense, the term points to a ritual type, to a genre of rites grounded in processes of negotiation aimed at settling something: a Catholic papal election, a Northwest Coast Potlatch, a *kaiko* pig festival in New Guinea, a nineteenth-century Yiddish wedding ceremony, a modern-day courtroom. The ritual frame of such these rites of negotiation must be flexible enough to allow for movement and shifting, yet solid enough to contain and ultimately resolve differences: a pope must be elected; the parents must agree on a contract; the jury must deliver a verdict.

One ritual type that can be imagined as a flexible container allowing for strategic negotiations is the tradition of Carnival, which explicitly includes reflexivity, critique, experimentation, and playfulness as integral features of the form. Carnival has been theorized as a "safety-valve" mechanism that merely seems to challenge a society's power structures; but it has also been described as a vehicle of critique, liberation, destruction, renewal, a "second-life" of the people. A more balanced view avoids the dualist either/or of these two theoretical perspectives, claiming that carnivalesque festivity is an arena or stage for the negotiation of identity, memory, beliefs, and values as well as political, economic, and sacred power.

Not only do certain ritual genres contribute to cultural and religious processes of negotiation, but the negotiating power of ritual and performance become especially important at certain sociohistorical moments, events Victor Turner referred to as "social dramas." Turner describes social processes in terms of patterned, dramatic action. A social drama unfolds when there is a breach of normative modes of social life that, if not sealed off or addressed, can lead to a state of crisis capable of splitting the social fabric into two or more contending groups. In response to this situation, redressive action arises—for instance, political debate, legal procedures, or military action. But Turner is particularly interested in the role of ritual and other genres of cultural performance as instruments of redress.

Ritual and performance are potentially liminal and reflexive. The term "liminality" derives from the Latin *limen*, literally, a threshold. A threshold or doorway mediates and joins two different spaces and has long been a symbol of transformation and change. In the social sciences, the concept of liminality has been developed and applied to practices associated with change, as well as ambiguous, fluid, and malleable moments or situations. If we tell someone, "take a good look in a mirror," we are suggesting (actually, imploring) that person to think about who they are, their behavior and actions, their lifestyle, their past actions, and their hopes and plans for the future. The mirror is a liminal and reflexive place. Redressive ritual is potentially transformative because of its liminal character. Ritual, for Turner, allows "the contents of group experiences [to be] replicated, dismembered, remembered, refashioned, and mutely or vocally made meaningful." If successful, redressive action leads to a reconciliation among the divided parties; if unsuccessful, it may fuel a crisis and lead to an irreparable breach, with a radical restructuring of social relationships as the inevitable result.

A fine example of Turner's notion of social drama is the Reformation. The drama of ritual and public performance propelled the German Reformation sparked by Martin Luther: there were protests in the streets, mock burnings of the pope, public debates, one of history's great trials (the Diet of Worms in 1521), the public burning of the papal bull calling for Martin Luther to recant, and, to top it all, the wedding of a defiant monk and a former nun (Luther and Katharina von Bora). Ultimately, the efforts to contain the Reformation through ritual channels—formal debates, legal and ecclesiastical penalties, trials—failed; Luther was excommunicated and the church split. If some ritual serves as a kind of stick that keeps society in order, other forms act as a crowbar or hammer to destabilize predominant values, identities, and beliefs. A history of social change from the perspective of changes to prominent rites and ceremonies remains to be written.

Don Handelman has proposed that much of the scholarly theorizing of ritual's relation to society can be placed in one of two camps, each employing a fundamental root metaphor. Handelman is most concerned about public events, larger-scale, collective performances. One theoretical approach, following the tradition of Durkheim, emphasizes the manner in which ritual *models* (and in so doing, establishes, reinforces, and legitimates) status quo values and social status systems and hierarchies. A model is a representation in miniature of some larger thing. A model airplane is a model of the real, functioning machine that flies. But a model may also be developed as a blueprint for the real thing; a new airplane design is first modeled and then built from the model. Similarly, ritual has this dual nature. An initiation rite, for example, is meant to model the values, know-how, and attitudes of adulthood; if successful, passage through the rite effects a change or transformation in the initiate. Handelman terms such rites "events that model."

A second slant to theorizing public ritual has utilized the metaphor of the *mirror*, but in two quite different senses. For Handelman, the mirror metaphor refers primarily to "events that present," those performative occasions in and through which a group presents itself to itself. Here, the function of the ritual "mirror" is, in good Durkhemian fashion, self-presentation, serving to solidify social order, both a model *of* and *for* society, as in the case of Venice's ducal processions. These are "events that present": events that legitimate that which they present.

Victor Turner, who took this tradition of structuralism with him into his fieldwork, stuck with the mirror metaphor, but he added to it the notion of public and plural *reflexivity*. If group celebration, for example, is a mirror held up to that group, it is not just passively reflecting social arrangements but also producing an image that can be seen, experienced, and reflected upon. In Turner's view, ritual need not be understood as a mere epiphenomenon of social structure—a view which privileges an abstract "society" over its more concrete manifestations—our rites and performances may also be vehicles of insight, resistance, and social change. Handelman refers to these as "events that re-present." Ritual in this view is like a piece of society, which society itself cuts out and offers to itself for inspection, reflection, and possibly criticism.

Ideas and attitudes about ritual's relation to society revolve around several dualities. Is ritual confirmatory action or creative force? Does ritual statically reproduce social structure or is it more processual, enacting the dynamics of social change? Do collective group rites generate the experience of solidarity or reinforce hierarchies and inequities? Is ritual deployed in the interests of solidifying power or is it an instrument of resistance? Historically in ritual studies, there was a sea change in theorizing ritual in the 1970s, as the work of Victor Turner and others pushed off of the structuralist tradition to highlight ritual's critical and creative potential. The point, of course, is not to come down in favor of one side of these dualities but to better understand the complex character of public ritual. There are rites that conserve, transmit, and protect tradition; others are creatively, critically, strategically employed to enact change. Although there is a tendency to praise creativity and change over conservation and tradition, rites need to be evaluated in their social contexts; change is not always for the better and tradition is not always oppressive.

Chapter 4
Ritual and transformation

Change is natural: the seasons come and go, butterflies emerge from larvae, and erosion grinds down mountains. That people change too is plain enough, aging and illness being obvious examples. But societies also create cultural forms and institutions designed to actively promote change, or to use a stronger, less naturalistic term, *transformation*. There are many rites that traffic in symbols and processes of transformation—healing rites, funerary rites, magic, sacrifice, rites of inversion, rites of passage. Sacrificial rites, for example, take a mundane thing or ordinary living being and consecrate it into something of value and potency.

Ritual is sometimes distinguished from technical, instrumental activity; yet ritual, too, aims to get things done. Yoking ritual to transformation is common in ritual studies. Here are few examples:

- Robbie Davis Floyd, well known for her studies of hospital birth, which she theorizes as a rite of passage, claims that ritual's "primary purpose is transformation."

- Tom Driver identifies "transformation" as one of the "three great gifts that ritual makes to social life," the other two being "establishment of order and the deepening of communal life."

- The recent volume of essays, edited by Don Handelman and Galina Lindquist, *Ritual in Its Own Right*, focuses on the "dynamics of transformation" in ritual.

- The anthropologist Anthony Wallace, writing in 1966, defined religion as a "set of rituals rationalized by myth, which mobilizes supernatural powers for the purpose of achieving or preventing transformations of state in man and nature."

To a results-oriented culture, for any activity to be of value it needs be useful. The discussion of ritual efficacy is partly driven by the valuing of utility in contemporary culture. Of course not all ritual is prized for its utility—a festival may have consequences, but it sounds odd to suggest we celebrate to accomplish something. Not all ritual is about work, power, and transformation. Giving praise is not really aimed at results—it is a shout of joy directed to the cosmos. Clearly, however, there are rites that do aim to accomplish some particular end. From the perspective of ritual practitioners, a healing rite aims to make the patient healthier, an exorcism to banish a possessing spirit or demon, a sacrifice to placate or curry favor with the gods. Ritual theorists also approach ritual as not merely decorous or expressive, but of real consequence and practical efficacy.

Since there are many rites aiming at some specific end, efficacy is one way in which ritual has been distinguished from other kinds of action. For example, consider Michael Houseman, who notes that "ritual action, if it is efficacious ... irreversibly affects ordinary intercourse in perceptible ways: before and after are not the same. From this point of view, ritualization is serious business, its efficacy quite different from the gratification that results from playing (or observing) a game or from observing (or participating in) a spectacle." Victor Turner makes a similar distinction, separating *ritual* in a narrow sense (defined by its transformative power), from *ceremony*, with its more socially conservative mood.

Transformations of the self through ritual means may be ontological, cognitive, biological, status-related, or combinations of these. Just what a rite precisely accomplishes will depend on who is asked. For the Navajo, a chantway rite restores harmony to the body, society, and cosmos. For an anthropologist partial to social functionalism, ritual keeps society in order. For a Marxist, ritual both actualizes and occludes social inequalities and class relations. What one sees depends on how one looks.

The questions informing the broad discussion of ritual's agency and efficacy are embedded in Houseman's "if it is efficacious." If ritual is efficacious, just how does it accomplish its work? What does it mean to say ritual exercises transformative power or force? How is the power of ritual generated and passed along to ritualists? Is ritual really capable of effecting transformation? Is ritual actually doing what either practitioners or scholars claim it is doing? Can ritual fail? Should a marriage end in divorce, is ritual at all responsible? In exploring these questions, let us focus on two categories of ritual commonly associated with change and transformation—initiation and magic.

Initiation

The word "initiation" is of Latin origin, and it refers to any ritual means of taking on a new role; literally a "beginning" or an "entrance." Taking an oath of office, for example, could be considered initiation, though such rites are usually classified as a case of "civil ritual," rather than a rite of passage. Initiatory rites are sometimes referred to as "status elevation rites," which suggests a working definition: initiation rites change an individual's status (or at least purport to change it). In scholarship, the term "initiation" is applied to a variety of ritual action. There are vocational rites (priestly ordination) and initiations into religious or monastic orders (the Zen Buddhist *Jukai* ceremony); initiation into secret societies (clan rites, the mystery traditions of ancient Greece, or the Masonic Lodge); rites that confirm membership in entire religious traditions (circumcision in Judaism or baptism in Christianity); and rites associated with entrance into adulthood. Discussion of initiation usually focuses on this later type, on how societies weave together the biological changes of adolescence with the attitudes and expectations of adulthood. Initiation, in the simplest and commonest use of the term, transforms boys into men and girls into women.

Initiation in this more restricted sense of "coming of age" exhibits shared family characteristics. Initiation involves mentorship and has a pedagogical dimension in which initiates generally assume a posture of obedience toward elders. Initiates are taught geography, stories, history, and myth, as well as practical knowledge and skills. Initiation rites often involve the infliction of pain, which is sometimes extreme, through vigils, fasting, body scarring or tattooing, beating, and the strict observance of taboos. Initiates are often separated from the social group, leaving the safety and familiarity of public and domestic spaces for the dangers and rigors of a secluded locale. Here, in this transitional space, initiates undergo trials and ordeals, often designed to create the experience of humiliation or intimidation, paradoxically coupled with an elevation in social or spiritual status. Deceptions and reversals of expectations, the revelation of sacred knowledge, the receiving of names, and exchange of gifts are typical of initiation rites.

In classifications of rites, initiation is considered—alongside marriage, funerary, and birth rites—as one of the "rites of passage," a phrase coined by Arnold van Gennep in his 1908 work of that name. Van Gennep was dissatisfied with how ritual had been treated by James Frazer, who was chiefly concerned with the formal meanings of rites and their relation to myth. The crux of ritual, claimed van Gennep, and of initiation in particular, is not meaning, but efficacy: initiation is principally an instrument for the transformation of an individual's social status. Van Gennep was pivotal in drawing attention to the sociocultural work conducted through ritual action. Ritual is not mere re-enactment of beliefs, narratives, or values but en-actment; a rite of passage does not simply mark a transition in the life cycle but affects it. Van Gennep advanced the reasonable idea that rites must be understood in their social contexts and argued that the elements of any particular rite need to be analyzed and understood in relation to the larger ritual systems in which they are embedded. Van Gennep also called for a "sequential method" that studied a rite in relation to both what preceded it and followed it.

Van Gennep's text is predominately concerned with initiation. Reading through ethnographic accounts of male adolescent rites in nonindustrial societies, van Gennep discerned a common pattern. A group of boys is separated from domestic space and their mothers, then taken to a sequestered, transitional zone where they endure ordeals and receive teachings that generate and mark their transition to adulthood. Upon their return, they are incorporated into the village as full-fledged men. Van Gennep called these stages in initiation rites separation, transition, and incorporation.

Both the life cycle of an individual and social organization are composed of a set or sequence of recognized status positions, and the task of initiation is to move people through these positions, which are generally age related. Van Gennep also imagined the life course as akin to the changing of the seasons. Movement through social positions is performed ritually via movement to and through a sequestered or extramundane location or territory, although sometimes passage may be purely symbolic. Social transformation is also accompanied by an inner transformation of state. The emphasis on passage, transition, and transformation in van Gennep's theorizing meant an emphasis on the middle stage of initiation, as this where transformation takes place. The transitional phase in initiation rites is a primary example of ritual liminality, that phase, stage, or moment of ritual in which the status of participants is ambiguous, in transition between two different social or ontological states.

In the end, van Gennep's thought can be seen as the extended elaboration of an analogy: a change or transformation of status or state is akin to movement through space. Presumably, even though he does not make this explicit, van Gennep holds that at the local level, the efficacy of passage rites is rooted in an analogy that when shared, dramatized, and performed turns into metaphorical identification. Just as a wedding ring does not represent marriage but *is* marriage, transition and transformation through initiation passage is the thing itself: if you do not "pass through" the ordeals, you do not become a man.

Victor Turner developed van Gennep's approach, emphasizing liminality as "the mother of all invention." An overturning or negation of formal categories, conventions, and social structures is characteristic of liminality. In Turner's hands, the passage model introduced by van Gennep was broadly applied to theater and ritual; in reading Turner, at times "ritual" and "drama" are used almost interchangeably. In his accounts of Ndembu ritual, Turner developed a symbolic approach, arguing that the efficacy of initiation and healing rites is found in the creative, dramatized deployment and relational clustering of symbols to bridge bodily experience with more abstract thought. The action or dynamics of ritual, in Turner's view, is a process of constructing, sometimes deconstructing meaning, beliefs, values.

Unusually, the Hopi are one of the few tribes that initiate boys and girls into adult as one age cohort. The rite takes place in February, a time of renewal when the Hopi celebrate the opening of the kivas (underground ceremonial spaces) and the return of kachinas (masked spirits, deities, or mythic beings) to the human world. Children are ritually whipped; an act which encourages secrecy. The following day, a culminating kachina dance takes place in the kiva, during which the dancers remove their masks, revealing to the children a startling truth: the kachinas are performed by the members of the community. Children see their kin in costume, an act that engenders a profound experience of confusion and disillusionment.

The children, as religious studies scholar Sam Gill puts it, are ritually "disenchanted." Hopi children regularly encounter the kachinas in ceremony, stories, and visual art, but as children they are guarded from perceiving the kachinas as masked figures. During their initiation, the "secret" is revealed, an event that constitutes transformation, not just socially but at an existential and ontological level. Coming of age, becoming an adult, deliberately coincides with a sense of disillusionment but also with access to the kiva and entry into Hopi religious life. The "experience," remarks Gill, "makes return to a previous way of life impossible." The children's initiation begins with intensifying a received understanding of reality, only to then pull the rug from beneath them. Being forced "to abandon one's ingrained notion of reality is to experience a true death of the former self." The task set for the new, adult member of the community is that of coming to a more nuanced and complex understanding of reality and Hopi religiosity.

How does initiation work? How does the performance of certain acts and utterances transform people? An ethologist (and certain proponents of "ecological" social theory) would answer by pointing to the mechanism of natural selection; to say ritual (or ritualization) works is to say that a particular behavioral repertoire has survival value. Some social scientific theory would say initiation works because of social convention—it works because we agree it does. Cognitive theorists would say that initiation works by re-orienting our mental categories and thought processes at a deep neurological level. Symbolists hold that ritual is composed of symbolic components that when woven together create a pattern or structure of meaning, perhaps like a spider's web. Performance theorists emphasize the dramatic phases in rites, and how these transitions enact, like in theater, moments of crisis and resolution. Van Gennep's passage model suggests the enactment of a strong metaphor. Most attempts at theory cobble together several of these notions. Gill's interpretation tacitly draws on the cognitive and experiential impact of dramatic, embodied performance. Hopi initiation works because it is powerful enough to shatter one's worldview.

Is an explanation for how ritual works really possible, or even really what we are after? Clifford Geertz once wrote: "Believing, with Max Weber, that man [*sic*] is an animal suspended in webs of significance he himself has spun, I take culture to be those webs, and the analysis of it to be therefore not an experimental science in search of law but an interpretative in search of meaning." Here, Geertz seems to make explaining and interpreting mutually exclusive. There is a tendency to view explanation as reductive and therefore somewhat coldhearted, while interpretation connotes greater sympathy. Whether this is actually the case is debatable. Interpretations, from the point of view of those being interpreted, can often be as inaccurate or as damaging as reductive explanation.

Ritual has so many different dimensions—biological, political, psychological, ecological, economic, religious—that a comprehensive, integrative explanation of its workings is likely forever beyond our grasp. Imagine writing an explanation for how a bicycle "works," and then multiply the difficulty a hundred- or a thousandfold. For this reason, theorizing ritual tends toward interpretation, and interpretation often tends toward the articulation of function, which in turn tends toward one-liners: ritual creates social bonds; ritual masks a society's asymmetrical power relations; ritual creates a subjunctive space for reflexivity. I tend to agree with Geertz that the study of ritual is largely a hermeneutical, rather than theoretical, endeavor. One way to avoid reductive kinds of interpretations is to offer detailed descriptions of ritual events, from their preparation, through enactment, and aftermath, while also situating rites in their sociohistorical contexts. In recent years, many such hermeneutical and performative studies of ritual have emerged, including my own *Performing the Reformation: Public Ritual in the City of Luther*. Ritual theory and the attempt to explain ritual efficacy will continue, but in the effort to generate comprehensive and systematic theories, scholarship will need to tend to more cross-cultural and comparative research, of which there is very little in the field of ritual studies.

Ritual criticism

In the 1980s, as cultural and critical theories rose to prominence, the theorizing of how ritual works gave way to critique of both theory and practice. Granted, ritual transforms. The new question was not so much how does it transform? but rather what are we to make of ritual transformations? The new direction was marked by Ronald Grimes's 1990 work *Ritual Criticism*, which called for examining the political and normative nature of rites and ritual theory, but also, following Victor Turner, for awareness of the critical dimensions of ritual—ritual itself as a way of doing criticism, encouraging reflexivity, and creatively responding to social and individual needs and concerns. In subsequent works, Grimes applied his notion of "ritual criticism" to the rising phenomenon of ritualizing passage rites (initiation, weddings, births, funerals) and problems associated with the appeal to classical rites of passage theorists—whose ideas were principally drawn from a selective reading of male initiation rites—for justification.

Vincent Crapanzano's work on Moroccan circumcision rites is a case in point. Crapanzano questions the assumptions of transformational models of initiation. The Moroccan rite "declares passage...[but] there is no passage whatsoever—only the mark of passage, the mutilation that is itself an absence, a negation." In Crapanzano's analysis, the rite creates not *communitas* but fear and submissiveness; it is not linear but circular; there is no actual transformation from boyhood to manhood. Circumcision does not move male children forward but simply returns them scarred (physically and emotionally) to the world of women. Van Gennep and other classical theorists gave little attention to the fact that initiation may be exploitive, and it may not always do what practitioners or even ritual theorists say it does. Purpose and function are not always neatly in synch. Transformation may be claimed, but not actualized.

Crapanzano's work exemplifies an attitude of suspicion toward initiation, critically examining the secrecy, deception, and violence found in many rites as tools in the maintenance of privilege and power. Is circumcision, for example, to be spoken of as "marking" or as "abuse"? Hazing rites, which tend to receive public condemnation, are a form of initiation. Hazing, which involves violence and acts of transgression, aims to inculcate submission to authority and build solidarity on a unique experience outside the bounds of social norms, an experience not to be revealed to a wider public. In this regard, hazing has similarities to the violence and secrecies of domestic abuse, where the victim, paradoxically enough, often remains loyal to the abuser. In hazing, shame and disgust are generated and then transformed by the ritual process into a dark loyalty, trust, and esprit de corps. In gangs and in military contexts, another function of hazing is to create the willingness and dispositions necessary to torture and kill human beings.

Robbie Davis-Floyd, in her analysis of the ritualization of hospital birth, argues that societies use life-cycle passages to literally inscribe their most fundamental values and assumptions into the body. Davis-Floyd treats the medical procedures of Western hospital birth as a principal initiation rite of modern Western culture, arguing that the literal openness of women during birth is the prime occasion for society to reinforce dominant values and beliefs on the bodies and minds of its members. In the case of hospital birth, these values are principally those of technocracy, efficiency, and a distrust of instincts and the body. Studying the exploitive and controlling nature of such secular initiations as hazing and hospital birth may lead us to a more critical view of the kinds of transformation taking place through initiatory practices.

Initiatory rites may indeed be transformative, but we must critically evaluate the kinds of transformations generated. Transformation is a potent and spiritually positive sounding word; but transformation need not be necessarily praised, and ritual transformations may be highly politicized acts through which oppressive power is wielded and maintained. Rather than assume ritual is an agent of transformation, or define it as such (as does Victor Turner), the posture of "ritual criticism" developed by Grimes and others asks us to describe more precisely the "before" and "after" states, in order to qualitatively measure and ethically evaluate the kinds of changes taking place in and through ritual.

Magic

There is a second class of ritual where questions of transformation and efficacy are prominent—magic. In everyday use, and in some scholarship, the term has a pejorative ring to it and typically connotes a sense of superstition. Magic is often identified in ritual studies as a broad category of ritual, including rites associated with hunting, exorcism, divination, fertility, spells, and healing. The term refers to a set of practices, the aim of which is to bring about certain changes or conditions in groups, individuals, or nature, where the changes are held to be the result of these acts. If you till the soil, fertilize, irrigate, and otherwise maintain a vegetable garden (agriculture), the chances of a successful harvest increase. But what happens should you sing, dance, and pray (ritual) over your tomatoes? Will this make any difference? This is a crude example, but it cuts to the core of the debate over the efficacy of magical rites and practices.

The English anthropologist E. B. Tylor claimed that magical thinking (the notion, say, that prayer has an effect on tomatoes) is "one of the most pernicious delusions ever vexed on mankind." Tylor understood magical thinking as a rational process, but horribly misguided. Performing a rain dance, for example, is based on a reasoning of sorts in which like produces like; the feet mimic the falling of rain on the ground in an effort to cause the actual falling of rain. The flaw is not in the logic, says Tylor, but in a very poor understanding of the kinds of outcomes capable of being produced by certain acts. Magic is a "primitive" kind of science—and it simply does not work. Magic eventuates in no transformative effects, in spite of what particular cultures may claim. In theories of cultural evolution, a society's penchant and commitment to "magic" marks a distinction between so-called primitive and civilized cultures. In the first half of the twentieth century it was fashionable (at least, among Western intellectuals) to think that cultures evolved by progressing from a worldview rooted in magic to one based on religion and finally to science.

The "intellectualist" school's understanding of magic has several problems, the least of which is its rhetoric of cultural dominance. But even on its own terms, the critical suspicion of magic leveled by Tylor, James Frazer, and others is on shakier ground when we consider rites associated with individuals and groups. It is obvious that you can influence someone's mood through means other than hitting them on the head with a hammer. Giving someone "the cold shoulder" is enough to produce changes in a relationship. There need be no physical contact whatsoever in bullying, yet bullying can have disastrous consequences. Can symbolic acts influence the course of events in the natural world, such as the weather or the course of a disease? This is a trickier question, though even here there are studies claiming that, for example, playing classical music positively impacts plant growth, when compared with playing rock music or no music at all. If music can alter conditions in the natural world, then perhaps prayer, dance, and song can as well?

The litmus test for the debate over ritual efficacy has been healing rites, sometimes referred to as "religiomagical" healing. Healing is a complex and diverse phenomenon. Many religious rites—pilgrimage, meditation, prayer, funerals, fasting—are fundamentally connected to healing. Services or rites of healing are central to the religious practice of some traditions, as is the case with Vodoon, the Navaho, and Christian Science. Other traditions incorporate healing into their ritual system and worldview, for example, the Christian practice of anointing the sick with oil, or the Buddhist use of medicinal metaphors in explicating the dharma. In popular culture and contemporary spirituality we find many practices implicated in processes of healing: yoga, tai chi, reiki, psychotherapy.

In the context of Western biomedicine, study after study demonstrates that the effectiveness of medical treatment is to be attributed to the so-called placebo effect. Medical doctors see large numbers of patients with nonspecific complaints. The logical structure or form shaping the visit to the doctor's office—examination, diagnosis, treatment, prognosis, the physician's authority, the patient's trust, the use of technology—is often enough to effect cure. And, in cases with specific complaints and identifiable organic diseases, a good portion of the treatment efficacy is attributable to the generalized form of what generally transpires in the medical setting. Western biomedicine, the presuppositions of which are not all that different from the intellectualist analysis of magic, is generally at a loss to account for these facts. In large measure, we can attribute the theoretical difficulties here to the mind–body dualism of Western thought: disease is a condition of the body, the reception and understanding of treatment and healing the provenance of the mind or soul, and biomedicine has no suitable categories to mediate between these binary oppositions.

The effort to explain and understand the efficacy of the placebo effect, Western biomedicine's own form of magic, generally points to the symbolic qualities common to both "modern" medical treatment and "traditional" healing rites. Falling ill and being healed involve interactions between patient, healer, family, community, and, in some cases, spirits, demons, or the sacred. These interactions are both instrumental (cleaning a wound, for example)—the physiological and pharmacological know-how present in traditional healing rites has long been underestimated—but also decisively symbolic and performative, providing a culturally sanctioned vocabulary, explanation, or narrative in making sense and effectively dealing with illness.

Given that the healing rites of the world's religions variously make use of dance, music, song, chant, stylized movement, utterance, and dramatic action, they are readily regarded as performances. Performance approaches to healing often emphasize the importance of process, embodiment, enactment, the senses, and aesthetics in creating or evoking "presence." The Navajo Blessing Way ceremony, for example, invokes and restores the presence of *Hozho*, usually translated as harmony or beauty. Furthermore, many cultures hold that illness is the result of disorder in social relations, and a cathartic resolution of disorder is often a dramatic affair. Turner in his study of the Ndembu, writes: "The sickness of the patient is mainly a sign that 'something is rotten' in the corporate body. The patient will not get better until all the tensions and aggressions in the groups interrelations have been brought to light and exposed to ritual treatment." Lastly, symbolic and performance models of healing often distinguish between sickness and illness on one hand, and curing and healing on the other. Sickness refers to biological disease, for example, cancer, while illness refers to the psycho-social-spiritual experience and meaning of disease, the "war against cancer." The etymology of the English verb "to heal" includes such meanings as "to make sound or whole" and "to restore to original purity or integrity." Healing is more comprehensive than curing; whereas curing is directed to bodily disease, healing (to use a Western image) involves body, mind, and spirit. Thus it is possible to be healed of cancer, yet die from the disease.

Unsettled issues

The symbolist school of thought, which emerged with full force in the work of Clifford Geertz, Victor Turner, and Stanley Tambiah, critiques the intellectualists' suspicions of the transformational power of magic and of ritual, more broadly, on two grounds. First, the "scientific" and "symbolic" are two different kinds of discourse, different conceptual systems, and magic should not be reduced to science and then compared with it on its terms. Second, it is rather obvious that acts we might terms "symbolic" or "magical" can have empirical outcomes in social and interpersonal lifeworlds. One way of defining magic is as the use of symbolic means to produce empirical effects. In this sense, magic is not restricted to "traditional" or "primitive" societies but is at work in the modern West, too: advertising ought to be proof of that.

Still, magic has proven a tough nut to crack in ritual theory. The most comprehensive effort to think through the history of theorizing of magic is Stanley J. Tambiah's *Magic, Science and Scope of Rationality*, published in 1990. Far from being merely a historical survey, Tambiah's goal is to investigate the categories, limits, and range of modern, Western rationality, as evidenced in ritual theory. In his discussion of the work of Bronislaw Malinowski, Tambiah emphasizes a "duality" or ambiguity in Malinowski's effort to make sense of the efficacy of Trobriand Islander ritual. Malinowski's understanding of ritual, says Tambiah, is characterized by a number of "unsettled issues." For Malinowski, Trobriand ritual "was 'objectively' false but… 'subjectively' true to the actors." Magic is psychologically, socially effective in terms of its pragmatic impact on people and groups, but not effective in any objectively causal, material sense. Western rationality divides the world into binary oppositions—object/subject, matter/spirit, reality/illusion—and then privileges the first term in these opposition. In such a worldview, magic (ritual efficacy more generally) works as a kind of illusion or psychosocial trick, but it does not "really" work, it is not "really" real—and around we go again, trying to illuminate the relationship between mind and body. Tambiah holds out hope for a grand theory capable of transcending the dualisms shaping ritual theory; approaches to ritual emphasizing performance and embodiment are one way of dealing with the dualisms Tambiah identifies.

Chapter 5
Definitions, types, domains

Is ritual a particular kind of action, or a quality of action potentially available in a variety of situations? If ritual is a particular kind of action, how it is to be defined? Is ritual perhaps not an actual phenomenon at all but rather a scholarly construct, an arbitrary way of ordering and classifying elements of our phenomenal world? How is ritual related to other domains of human action, such as theater, sports, play, or work? Are there different kinds of ritual, just as there are different genres of literature? Such are the vexed questions of ritual theory.

Reading through the vast scholarship on ritual, we see the word "ritual" used in three different, though related, ways. First, ritual is conceived as a kind or variety of action. When people act in a specified way, they are said to be engaging in ritual. Here, ritual theory proceeds by stipulating ritual's unique, formal features. Second, ritual appears in scholarship as a cultural domain, arena, stage, or field, in and out of which people act and are acted upon. In this approach, ritual is both related to and different from other cultural domains the likes of play, theater, and sports. In thinking about historical and cultural dynamics, ritual is sometimes presented as an ideal type, a modality of interaction and engagement with the world. Third, ritual is sometimes conceived as an actor in its own right. Ritual as a medium has force, power, efficacy, or agency. Examining ritual's various functions, trying to understand how ritual accomplishes its works, has received a good deal of attention.

Alongside these various usages, many scholars question the analytical value of the concept of "ritual," since the term has so many different meanings and uses. Others have suggested that ritual is little more than a scholarly invention, an empty signifier pointing to no identifiable object. Catherine Bell's work is widely recognized as a major contribution to ritual studies, yet her overall project is to call into question the very notion of ritual. Ritual, she claims, "is not an intrinsic, universal category or feature of human behavior," and "ritual as such does not exist." The challenge in conceptualizing ritual is navigating between two rather extreme positions. On one hand, ritual can be so broadly defined as to find it everywhere; on the other, some scholars deny ritual any reality at all: ritual exists both everywhere and nowhere.

Recent research challenges critics like Bell who argue that the idea of ritual is analytically weak or little more than an act of conceptual colonization. Michael Stausberg has suggested, through a survey of emic equivalents to the word "ritual" in a wide variety of languages and cultures, that the basic assumption of ritual studies—"rituals can be found in each and every society, culture and religion"—bears weight. By ritual, Stausberg means a demarcated domain of sociocultural life: "different cultures...seem to 'refer' to a specific domain of life that we, in the West, happen to denote by the term 'ritual.'" His conclusion is that although "ritual" is indeed a modern Western notion, this idea of ritual (in a manner similar to its emic equivalents in other cultures) draws together a cluster of interrelated actions, beliefs, and values: order, precepts, laws, prescriptions; customs, morals, habits; actions, performance, work; worship, honoring, assembling; secret knowledge, memorization, intentions; marking off, separating, elevating.

The word "ritual," in other words, does carve out an object of study, though its edges are somewhat fuzzy.

Definitions of ritual are legion. Let us briefly consider an oft-cited one, proposed by Victor Turner. For Turner, ritual is "formal behavior prescribed for occasions not given over to technological routine that have reference to beliefs in mystical beings or powers." Definitions can be useful. Definitions focus attention on a particular feature or issue of interest, but they are typically fraught with limitations. Turner's definition, we note, makes all ritual religious. But is a parade ritual? A courtroom trial? A graduation ceremony? None of these make reference to mystical beings or powers, yet there are good reasons for counting each of them as ritual. And, as far as religious ritual goes, Turner's definition emphasizes theism ("mystical beings") and animism ("powers") to the exclusion of all other varieties of religion.

Second, Turner suggests that ritual action is yoked to belief. Again, we may ask, does a bar mitzvah require "belief in mystical beings"? Likely not. Here, Turner falls into a foundational dualism of Western thought and culture, that beliefs (or thoughts or ideas or words) are primary, while actions, deeds, gestures, are derivative. Moreover, the notion of belief is today so laden with literalism and an objectivist epistemology that Turner's definition fails to do justice to those rites characterized by a subjunctive mood, ludic playfulness, and imagination, qualities of much ritual that Turner himself was drawn to in his research. Does a Hopi performing a kachina dance "believe" he is a kachina? The implied ontology here lacks nuance and sophistication. Moreover, many ritual traditions emphasize participation or observance over belief.

Third, the phrase "not given over to technological routine" suggests that ritual is chiefly noninstrumental; this may be the case for celebrations and festivals, which are expressions of collective joy (though even these events have practical outcomes), but rites classified as "magic" are meant to have explicitly empirical results. A Navajo healing ceremony aims to heal, so it seems appropriate in such cases to speak of a technology of ritual. Oddly enough, Turner's definition of ritual betrays the sense of ritual that pervades much of his writing, a warning sign about the limits of definitions.

Family resemblances

Since definitions can be limiting, we find in the social sciences and humanities other ways of demarcating a field of study. One of the more common approaches was developed by Ludwig Wittgenstein. In his *Philosophical Investigations,* Wittgenstein proposed a "family resemblance" approach to classifying games. Since there is no single or even one set of elements that all games necessarily and sufficiently share, the best we can do is describe the generally shared features and qualities of games. What Wittgenstein said of games is true of ritual: we are dealing with "a complicated network of similarities overlapping and crisscrossing." Wittgenstein then compared this network of shared characteristics to the resemblances found in families; it may be that two members of a family share no discernible traits in common and yet still be part of the same family by virtue of being linked through affinities with other family members. Critics would argue that once one starts making a list of features, the more ambiguous and slippery the notion of ritual becomes, and hence analytically weak. My view is that family resemblances are the best we can do when it comes to delineating what ritual is, and this is because ritual is as much a quality or style of action, rather than a single, distinct thing. Because of the interdisciplinary nature of ritual studies, family resemblance approaches to ritual tend to predominate. Whatever strategy one adopts—formal definition or family traits—the important point is how and to what extent these strategies are employed to reveal different modes of ritual experience.

Our attitude toward definitional and conceptual issues is partly shaped by metaphysical assumptions. Are universal categories in some sense real, or in positing them do we force the irreducibly particular nature of reality into made-up constructs? Does a healing rite have anything in common with the Olympic Games, other than our conceptual and imaginative ability to lump them together under a metacategory of "ritual"? The debate here is not merely epistemological and ontological, but political. One of Catherine Bell's concerns is to highlight how categorizing and classifying—central features of the Western intellectual tradition—have been instruments of colonial thinking and imperialism. In the case of ritual studies, there is a truth to this critique, since much early work involved Western scholars studying the rites of "primitive" societies as part of the effort to construct theories of cultural evolution.

Bell stands in the tradition of Michel Foucault, for whom definition and classification are forms of violence and dominance. In this sense, "practice theorists" like Bell argue that ritual studies is partly like ritual itself—both are strategic means of exercising power. Bell's mistake, in my view, is that even should ritual have no essence, it does not follow that the category has no legitimacy. Too often scholarship on ritual has forced a false either-or choice between essentialism and the entirely arbitrary. Wittgenstein's family resemblance approach offers a way through this dualistic thicket, bridging the gap between difference and identity.

Ritualization, rite, ritual

Rather than speak of ritual, per se, which connotes a stable, fixed thing, some theorists employ the notion of *ritualization*. In ethology, ritualization refers to a process of stylization and formalization in which instrumental behavior becomes symbolic and communicative. It is not difficult to find analogues of this process in human ritual. Consider, for example, a Communion service. The eating of bread, an instrumental act (we eat to survive), is transformed into a communicative behavior in the enactment of the Eucharist. The liturgy develops stylized and stereotyped acts and utterances independent of the consumption of food, and these serve to communicate narratives, attitudes, and values; the liturgy is conducted in a set-aside space (a church), and is accompanied by special dress (robes) and symbolically laden objects (candles, images), the human equivalent of specialized body parts and bright colors, to enhance its effectiveness. Through the act of Communion people establish and regulate identities and relationships to human and other than human beings.

We have then three concepts that are ideally distinguished from one another, though their usage tends to overlap: ritualization, rites, and ritual, a terminology first introduced by Ronald Grimes. Formally identifiable rites grow out of the *ritualization* of everyday life. In baptism, the simple act of washing becomes, through ritualization, associated with spiritual purification, regeneration, and renewal. In meditative traditions, sitting is ritualized into awareness. In sacrifice, butchering an animal is ritualized into an offering to the gods, a gesture of thanksgiving, an act of appeasing and placating higher powers. A formal *rite* entails a sequence or sequences of actions rendered special within an community or tradition by virtue of their elevation and stylization, generally named and set off from ordinary behavior by virtue of their being localized in special places and performed at special times. A bar mitzvah, a white wedding, a Catholic confirmation, a Hindu puja—these are nameable, observable rites. The notion of *ritual* is a more general and abstract attempt to identify what particular rites or groups of rites have in common.

The life of aristocrats in tenth-century Japan, the Heian period, was highly ritualized, as evidenced by the "Testamentary

Admonitions," written by the statesman and courtier Fujiwara no Morosuke:

> Upon arising, first of all repeat seven times in a low voice the name of the star of the year. Take up a mirror and look at your face, to scrutinize changes in your appearance. Then look at the calendar and see whether the day is one of good or evil omen. Next use your toothbrush and then, facing West, wash your hands. Chant the name of the Buddha and invoke those gods and divinities whom we ought always to revere and worship. Next make a record of the events of the previous day. Now break your fast with rice gruel. Comb your hair once every three days, not every day. Cut your fingernails on a day of the Ox, your toenails on a day of the Tiger. If the day is auspicious, now bathe, but only once every fifth day.

Here, religious practices (fasting and chanting) mix and mingle with matters of personal hygiene and self-reflection. Ritual is typically distinguished as special, non-ordinary behavior, so domestic life—toothbrushing, say—is generally not understood as ritual, because it is too quotidian. This passage, however, demonstrates two important points in the study of ritual. First it shows us how ritual is put together. Just as theater takes the drama of everyday life, condenses it, formalizes it, and puts it on stage for view, ritual is cobbled together out of ordinary acts and gestures made extraordinary; this cobbling together is the process of ritualization. Second, it demonstrates that any behavior can be ritualized; through ritualization mere behavior is transformed into action. Morosuke's morning routine is more than simple routine. It is in the articulation of this "more" that we begin to see what is unique about ritual.

The ritualization of action is accomplished through a variety of means. A short list, with reference to Morosuke's morning practices, would include the following:

- Repeating the action (perform each morning; repeat seven times)
- Prescribing and regularizing the details (next do this; next do that)

- Linking and elevating the action by associating it with sacred values, narratives, or figures (chant the name of the Buddha)
- Frame the action temporally, in terms of symbolic or historical time (in the name of the star of the year; look at the calendar)
- Invoke powers or figures to whom reverence, respect, honor is due (divinities whom we ought always to revere and worship)
- Perform the action with a special attitude (look at your face; reflect)

It may make sense to speak of degrees of ritualization. An action is more like ritual the more it is formalized, stylized, and aesthetically elevated through gesture, music, art, and performance; the more it receives spatial and temporal framing; the more it is associated with sacred powers, founding figures, or historical or mythic events.

The problem here is that doing more doesn't necessarily make for more ritual. In fact, sometimes doing less is what is called for. Ritualization may proceed by building up, repeating, and elevating, but also through a stripping down or singularizing of action. In meditative traditions, simply following one's breath is ritualized action; in Quaker meeting houses, silence, simplicity, and aesthetic minimalism reign supreme. Is a Quaker meeting less of a ritual than an ornate Anglican Communion service?

Types and domains

If ritual understood as a broad category of human action is a fuzzy concept, rites, as nameable practices, are easily identifiable. People continue making pilgrimages to shrines, prostrating themselves in mosques, taking oaths of office, marrying and burying. The question of defining ritual is linked to the challenge of classifying the diversity of rites we find enacted around the globe. Identifying ritual types or genres is helpful, since ritual is such a large category. Sometimes, ritual is treated as if it were of a piece. But clearly, there exists different kinds of ritual; what we conclude about one kind may not easily apply to other types.

Classification efforts have been a persistent feature of the study of ritual. Again, as with the effort to define ritual, we can find a range of attempts to devise a ritual taxonomy. One such list might include sacrifice, rites of passage, magic, secular ritual, interaction ritual, and seasonal rites. The problem is immediately apparent: the categories overlap, and it is not clear what criteria (duration, function, intention) are to be used to establish subcategories. Typologies are useful, however, insofar as they allow us to perceive similarities and differences among the variety of ritual, to focus attention on qualities or functions of interest, and to inform the effort to work out the center and boundaries of ritual action.

When Julian Huxley wrote his pathbreaking work on the behavior of the Crested Grebe in the years before the First World War, he had no qualms writing about "domestic dramas" and "ceremonies." Huxley would often compare his field observations with theater. In describing, for example, the "postnuptial" ceremony of a pair of Crested Grebes, he likened it to "the little run made by MacHeath and Polly in the 'Beggar's Opera.'" Flights of comparative imagination are not unusual in ritual studies. Huxley's language demonstrates that reflection about the nature and function of ritual relies on comparison and categorization.

Just what *is* ritual? Answering this question is more than a matter of definition. It requires tending to the diverse variety of ritual genres or types, as well as exploring the relationship between ritual and related genres of action. Thinking about ritual in terms of domains asks us to consider the ways in which ritual is both similar to and distinct from play, games, theater, or sports. Domain thinking is an analytical and comparative tool; it also alerts us to the ways in which ritual interacts with other domains in different cultures or across historical periods.

5. In this painting by Francisco Goya, matadors in a divided bullring prepare to deliver the final blow, as the audience leans in, drawn by the power of the spectacle. The tradition of bullfighting exemplifies the connections between ritual, theater, and sport.

Just as any act can be ritualized, we can imagine a range of behavior in various sociocultural domains through the lens of ritualization. Is the doffing of one's hat, or shaking hands, or holding the door open for someone, ritual? Are these not rather in the domain of habits, customs, and manners? The sociologist Erving Goffman employed the language of ritual in dealing with the daily multitude of face-to-face occasions in which matters of deference and demeanor play a crucial, if largely unconscious role. In developing his sociology of ordinary behavior, Goffman reached for the language of ritual, because even ordinary, informal, secular behavior, he realized, is filled with acts of symbolic communication. In the immediate presence of an object (human or material) of special value or importance, argues Goffman, we conduct ourselves in such a way as to guard or craft the communicative, symbolic implications of how we act. Ritualization ranges across a spectrum of cultural domains.

What Goffman accomplished for our understanding of "interaction ritual," bringing manners and habits into the world of ritual, Johann Huizinga accomplished for the study of play. Like play, ritual is a way of framing activity, and hence contextual. Huizinga, in his influential *Homo Ludens: A Study of the Play Element in Culture* (1944) explores the relationship between play and ritual. Both activities, he notes, transpire through an intricate framing of space:

> Just as there is no formal difference between play and ritual, so the "consecrated spot" cannot be formally distinguished from the play-ground. The arena, the card-table, the magic circle, the temple, the stage, the screen, the tennis court, the court of justice, etc., are all in form and function play-grounds, i.e. forbidden spots, isolated, hedged round, hallowed, within which special rules obtain. All are temporary worlds within the ordinary world, dedicated to the performance of an act apart.

A problem with this line of thinking is that it includes so much that we are left wondering where the "ordinary world" ends and the extraordinary world begins. After all, work, too, is a set-aside space where special rules obtain. Since play is Huizinga's superordinate category, he concludes that ritual is play, but not all play is ritual. Ritual, he suggests, is play that has become in some sense real, true, and believed.

Liturgy, or religious ritual

There is perhaps something to Huzinga's observation, and it has been developed by others. Don Handleman, building on the work of Mary Douglas and Gregory Bateson, has devised a theory of ritual around the notion of *framing*. Different activities are constituted by the "frames" we give them; inside or within a particular frame—a circus ring, a playground, a sports field, a theater, a temple—there is constituted a unique sets of rules, expectations, and attitudes. A crucial difference between play and ritual is that within the play frame, argues Handleman, messages and gestures are understood to be fictive, if not actually false: the child waving a wand is not Harry Potter, and that child knows it. Within the ritual frame, in contrast, messages are conceived and understood to be somehow true and real; another way to put this is that the ritual frame articulates that which is taken to be of ultimate, foundational, and fundamental value. In the West, ritual is often associated with high seriousness, and thus far from play. Many traditions around the world include rites that are playful and improvisational. In either case, however—ritual as serious business or ritual as play—the difference maker between ritual and play is the metamessage associated with each. The metamessage of ritual is that everything within the ritual frame is sanctified, true, real, and believed. One name given to such a ritual frame is *liturgy*.

It makes good sense to distinguish religious ritual from ritual more generally. If we use the term *rite* to refer to distinct, recognized ritual practices, usually enacted at specific times, in special places, we can point to religious rites by virtue of their place of enactment (a church, a mosque, a temple). If a rite is religious in this sense of placement, we may speak of *liturgy*. Political ritual and civil religion, in contrast, are often referred to as *ceremony*, in part because they take place in different kinds of spaces. The term "liturgy" is generally associated with Christianity and hence its use may involve bias and even religious imperialism. In spite of potential shortcomings, the term is common in ritual studies.

Liturgy is a nameable rite, a type of ritual, and a concept in ritual theory. Religious traditions organize their ritual practices in systems, and the liturgical system of most religious traditions is based on a central rite. In Christian traditions, it is common to speak of "the liturgy," usually with reference to Holy Communion. In the Lutheran and Anglican traditions, to consider only two examples of many, the liturgical system is based on the saving word of God and the sacraments of baptism (a one-time event) and Communion.

A Communion service consists of four phases: gathering, word, meal, and sending. The liturgy is opened by calling the community together via a musical prelude, a confession of faith, a greeting, and daily prayer. A series of readings follow. Usually there are two "lessons," drawn from the Hebrew Bible and New Testament epistles, plus a Gospel reading. These readings are interwoven with the singing of a psalm, hymns, a sermon, the recitation of the creed and prayers. Readings are structured according the seasons and festivals of the church year. The service of the meal consists of offerings, thanksgiving, the eating of bread and drinking of wine, and a communion hymn and prayer. The liturgy concludes with a blessing, a final hymn, and a musical postlude. Within the liturgical cycle of the church, the liturgy is adapted to suit the occasion. These occasions may be an ordinary Sunday, principal and lesser festivals, or services that take place in conjunction with passage rites: baptisms, weddings, confirmations, and funerals. In the Christian tradition, in addition to the main festival of Sunday celebrating the resurrection and redemptive work of Christ, the church year revolves through a cycle of greater and lesser festivals.

Liturgy is interrogative and declarative; it attempts to answer ultimate questions by stating—in words and gestures, through objects and images, via song and dance—how things are. Both spatial and temporal framing are usually of central importance to liturgy. Liturgy involves paradigmatic words and gestures typically linked to events deemed foundational by a particular tradition: the Jewish Passover, the enlightenment of the Buddha, the gift of the Koran to Muhammad, the Last Supper of Jesus with his disciples. Liturgy appeals to and invokes the past and tradition. That the word "tradition" is often used as a synonym for "religion" means that liturgy is the product of historical development and historical forces that set constraints on rapid changes in form and function.

Caroline Humphrey and James Laidlaw, in *The Archetypal Actions of Ritual,* divide ritual into two broad classes: shamanism and liturgy. Shamanism is rooted in the enactment of a convincing, theatrical-like performance, before an audience, an audience that needs in some fashion to be convinced by the performance. Liturgy, in contrast, entails doing things in precisely the right fashion, in a setting where everyone is a participant. In shamanistic or magical rites, the focus is on efficacy, on how well the rite works; in liturgy, the focus is on getting it right, enacting the rite in a formal, standardized way. Of course, in thinking about types, the ritual pie can divide into more than two pieces. The point Humphrey and Laidlaw are making however is that in many kinds of rites (which they refer to as liturgy), the emphasis is on a communal, shared enactment of gestures and utterances, and deployment of objects and symbols, the form of which come to us from outside ourselves. Such actions are "archetypal," not in the sense of deriving from some deep inner principle in the psyche but from the fact they are inherited or received from tradition. Liturgy has a pre-existing form, and ritualists aim at repeating, replicating, or entering into these pre-existing, elemental actions. What this means is that a participant in ritual is, in an important way, not the author of his or her own actions.

Such an "action-centered" conception of ritual is common. Ritual is not chiefly communicating meaning, a way of expressing what is already believed or valued in someone's head and heart; rather the action itself is central. Ritualized action is characterized by acts not constituted by the participant's intentions, but by prior stipulation and tradition. On one hand, participating in a rite demonstrates commitment, intention, belief, and one's solidarity with others. On the other hand, in participating, the ritual actor relinquishes agency; one is no longer the author of one's own acts but conforms to the form and elements that comprise the rite. For these theorists of ritual's archetypal features, handing over of agency is the core quality of the ritual frame.

Somewhat surprisingly, in the notion of ritual developed by Humphrey and Laidlaw, action is ritual action by virtue of a commitment to not be the author of one's own acts. The interesting feature of their approach is that it utilizes the dynamic relationship between action and intention as a tool to analyze and classify different kinds of behavior. Much of our everyday behavior makes sense only within the context of communicating meanings and intentions. If I shout, "Don't touch the pot; it's hot," I have a clear message or intention informing the action: I do not want you to burn your hand. Everyday action makes sense only if premised on the assumption that what we do is an expression of our intentional and emotional state. A different kind of dynamic arises when this premise breaks down, or is perceived to break down. Someone who feigns being upset by shedding tears is engaging in a certain kind of action—deception—which works (or fails) to the degree that we perceive or experience a fit between intentions and acts.

Ritual conceived as liturgy is yet another particular kind of relationship between actions and intentions, very much the reverse of everyday behavior. Ritual is a different way of framing or paying attention to the connections between what one is doing and what one is thinking or feeling. In ritual, it is the doing of the rite that is primary. Ritual is not an expression of intentions, motivations, feelings, beliefs, and so on; rather, ritual entails engaging in specific, formalized acts, and utterances not of one's own making. The actions are nonintentional in the sense that they come to us from outside ourselves, inherited, received, elemental, archetypal. Liturgy has a digital quality to it; you either do it or not. Unlike, say, sports, where one can play a good game one week and perform poorly the next, liturgy either happens or not; on or off. If you overthrow the receiver, playing poorly, you are still playing the game. But if the host is not consecrated in a Communion service; if the wedding ring is forgotten at home; if the young man refuses to read from the Torah at bar mitzvah—in such cases we have not a poorly executed rite but rather no rite at all.

What do we gain in conceiving ritual as liturgy (or as archetypal action)? For one, it places limits on understandings of ritual that emphasize communicative meaning. When we assume ritual is a medium of communicating, or a system of symbols, it becomes one among many such mediums, and we locate ritual in terms of a realm of meaning and signification that precedes and surrounds it: we reduce ritual to something other than itself. Second, the liturgical dimension of ritual allows us to broaden our notion of agency. Normally, we think of agency as being located in individuals, having to do with matters of will, intentionality, choice, desire. But there is a wider, distributed agency at work in ritual. We might be tempted to say a ritualist is merely "going through the motions," by which we suggest a distance between inner conviction and outward form. We assume here a relationship between intentions and actions, which mirrors that of the everyday world, and that ritual is inauthentic or ineffective if our heart is not really behind what we are doing. Agency, meaning, and efficacy all rests with us. But what if ritual action itself has the potential and power to impact one's intentions, emotions, feelings, and beliefs?

Chapter 6
Ritual as performance

In an essay on ritual, the anthropologist Edmund Leach writes: "Human actions can serve to *do* things, that is, alter the physical state of the world (as in lighting a bonfire), or they can serve to *say* things." For Leach, the more the action heads in the direction of *saying* something, the more easily we recognize the workings of ritual; the more an action is associated with *doing*, the farther we move away from ritual. For Leach, ritual is a form of symbolism, a way of communicating without the use of words. And, for Leach, ritual mainly communicates about already existing power relations in society. There are, however, many theorists of ritual who take the opposite approach, arguing that action is ritual by virtue of its efficacy. Michael Houseman, for example, emphasizes that in ritual "before and after are not the same." For Houseman, ritual is identifiable precisely because it is a "doing" action, not a "saying" action.

The British philosopher of language J. L. Austin provided a step toward a better understanding of ritual as a vehicle of transformation. Austin made the simple observation that through language we not only communicate information and develop propositions about the world—we actually accomplish things. When I say, "I promise to give the gift to your brother," I am not describing something—I am engaging in the act of making a promise. Austin called such utterances "speech acts," distinguishing them from purely indicative statements. When a priest utters, "I now pronounce you husband and wife," or, to use one of Austin's examples from his influential *How to Do Things with Words* (1962), a friend says, "I will bet you sixpence it will rain tomorrow," we are dealing with "performative sentences." In such cases, "to utter the sentence…is not to describe my doing…it is to do it." In *How to Do Things* Austin cuts through the binary opposition between saying and doing, examining cases "in which to say something is to do something; or in which by saying or in saying something we are doing something."

Austin made a significant, if indirect, contribution to the study of ritual: even should we conceive of ritual with the aid of linguistic metaphors, saying does not preclude action: saying and doing, communicating and acting need not be conceived as oppositional categories. Austin also helped encourage the development of a new kind of vocabulary and conceptual framework that would emerge through the 1980s under the rubric of "performance theory."

Performance theory emerged in part as a corrective to the conception of ritual in traditions of structuralism and social-functionalism. In performance theory there is an emphasis on ritual's dramatic and aesthetic qualities. Ritual often involves expressive action and heightened emotion, brought to life through a range of media—music, dance, and the visual arts. Performance theory seeks a better understanding of the relations between embodiment and knowing. Embodiment refers to the way in which intentions, feelings, beliefs, and values are not merely in the head but are bodily experiences. Ritual, as bodily action, is a way of knowing the world, and the kinds of ways the body is used is constitutive of our subjectivity and ideas. Performance approaches to ritual recognize its intersection with cultural domains (play, theater, sports, politics, and tourism), and recognizes both the creative and oppressive potential of ritual.

Some theorists of ritual (Catherine Bell, for example) critique the performance approach as falling down the slippery slope of analogy. Yet, applied to ritual, "performance" is far less metaphorical than is "text." Cross-culturally, ritual typically includes elements commonly associated with performance events: music or rhythmic accompaniment; dance or other stylized bodily movements; masking, costuming, and makeup. Ritual traditions and performance traditions often influence one another. In the nineteenth century, for example, evangelical Christianity in the northeastern United States incorporated into church architecture auditorium-style seating with a prominent stage, marquee lights, proscenium arches, and opera boxes; these changes to sacred space were shaped by and in turn encouraged a more theatrical and expressive liturgy.

Both the idea and traditions of performance have received a bad rap in Western culture since the Reformation. In the wake of the Reformation many European cities witnessed the closing of theaters and the suppression of theatrical and expressive genres such as carnival, puppetry, and opera. The sociologist Richard Sennett has discussed how during the Enlightenment the complexities of social interactions in salons, coffee houses, and other public places were replaced with an emphasis on the private sphere, personal authenticity, and a more isolated sense of one's self. Conceptually, "performance" has had an equally rough ride; we typically carry with us an ambivalent attitude toward performance. The verbs "to perform" or "to act" mean "to do" but also "to pretend," and so performing and acting are often thought of as being filled with pretense, particularly when associated with ritual. Ritual is serious business; it is not a mere performance, not mere play. But "to pretend" has other meanings: to intend; to design; to plot; to attempt; to hold before one; to extend. We need not divorce the serious, or the even sacred, from performance. To speak of human action in terms of performance is not to imply either fakery or lack of authenticity.

Performance studies is closely associated with the work and thought of Richard Schechner, who is both theater director and theorist; he was for many years the editor of the *Drama Review*. Through the 1970s and early 1980s, Schechner wrote several essays developing the ideas that would give shape to performance theory as an interdisciplinary field, encouraging and mingling with the thought of others in re-orienting the study of ritual. We can better understand what is at stake in Schechner's approach to ritual, and develop some aspects of his thought, with reference to a particular rite, the kōan tradition of Zen Buddhism.

Zen kōans

Kōans are pithy, enigmatic exchanges between master and disciple: What is the sound of one hand clapping? Kōans may be understood as psycholinguistic riddles aimed at frustrating discursive thought and hence capable of generating a certain type of experience. Kōans have also been framed and studied as a literary genre with a complex history embodying centuries of religious and philosophic discourse. These psychological and textual perspectives have dominated the study of the kōan tradition. Kōans, however, also hold a prominent place in the ritual system of Zen. Given that kōans are staged, worked on, enacted, watched, and judged, it makes sense to think of them as performances.

The word kōan originally meant something like "public document" or "public case." Each kōan presents the monk or student with a case to which a past master has given a precedent setting solution or answer or, perhaps more accurately, an embodied response. In Japan, the origins of kōan practice are found in the medieval period, roughly from 1300 to 1600 CE, where kōans developed as a kind of catechism: known responses to paradigmatic exchanges between master and disciple came to be performed as part of Zen training. The rise of kōan Zen in Japan coincides with the flowering of Nō theater under the leadership of the distinguished performer-playwrights Kan'ami and his son Zeami. These ritual and performance genres, if not directly influencing one another, were being shaped by cultural attitudes toward embodied, dramatic forms of enactment. Later, Hakuin Ekaku, as part of his efforts to revitalize monastic practice in Japan in the seventeenth century, established a graded kōan curriculum of some two hundred kōans, which form the basis of contemporary kōan practice in Japanese Rinzai Zen.

The first kōan encountered in contemporary kōan practice is typically Hakuin's One Hand: "In clapping both hands a sound is heard; what is the sound of the one hand?" Hakuin's One Hand has a formally accepted answer, outlined in a text that takes a few minutes to read. In response to the original question the student, as Yoel Hoffman revealed in his book of kōan scripts, "faces his master, takes a correct posture, and without a word, thrusts one hand forward." As the script proceeds, the student responds to questions with quotations from poetry and other Zen texts, engaging in verbal and bodily sparring, slipping through traps set by the master. While this kōan is relatively short, it may take months to develop an adequate response.

Zeami, in a treatise titled "Teaching on Style and the Flower," raises the question of the relationship between text and performance, and in doing so points to the value and function of performance. "What is the relation between movement and text in a Nō performance? Answer: This matter can only be grasped through intricate rehearsal.... [O]ne must project feelings that are in accord with the words being spoken.... When the idea of observing some object is suggested in the text, the actor performs a gesture of looking...when a sound is to be heard, the actor assumes an attitude of listening."

A similar dynamic can be detected in the script of Hakuin's One Hand. For example, at one point the master asks, "the Mt.-Fuji-summit-one-hand, what is it like? Answer: The pupil, shading his eyes with one hand, takes the pose of looking down from the summit of Mt. Fuji and says, 'What a splendid view!'

naming several places to be seen from Mt. Fuji—or others would name places visible from where they happen to be." Kōans are catechisms, of sorts; only the term "catechism" suggests rote responses to questions of doctrine or dogma. Kōans are perhaps better understood as scripts or scenarios, rather than as purely formulaic responses. A kōan text provides teacher and student with a script as the basis for ritualized performance.

Schechner refers to ritual (and theater, as well) as "restored behavior" or "twice behaved behavior," by which he means behavior that is both repetitious and rehearsed. When we engage in ritual, we are re-enacting prior performances. During a wedding, people act on the basis of explicit and tacit scenarios. Weddings, unlike funerals, are actually rehearsed, and weddings are embellished with ornate staging and presentation. Wedding photographs often reveal an element of show and putting-on for the occasion. Some forms of ritual head in the direction of theater; and some rites, like the Zen kōan, make the restoration of behavior an important, if not central, feature of the performance.

Ritual that emphasizes restored behavior is marked by reflexivity. Kōans, to stick with our example, are enacted over and over again until done right, and then one moves onto the next kōan in the curriculum. Schechner argues that ritual efficacy depends not just on ritual as an action or a doing but on ritual as "a showing of a doing." For Schechner, ritual has a kind of fictive or contrived quality. For precisely this reason, ritual actors create a distance between themselves and their doings, facilitating reflexivity. Ritual performance involves display, it is meant to be observed, the ritual act is shown to someone, even if that someone is an internalized self; and a rite is not necessarily a one time, static event, but, as is the case with kōan practice, an ongoing, dynamic affair.

Schechner's notion of ritual as a form of restored behavior fits some rites better than others; it has its limits and shortcomings. For one, ritual "actors" do not generally think of themselves as putting something on display or show, in the sense that a theater troupe might. Ritualists are not showing their doings, but simply doing. Second, there are many rites that are explicitly not meant to be seen—a papal election, for example. Last, the language of performance may suggest fakery or pretending at work in ritual, especially in the Western intellectual and religious traditions, where performance has somewhat of a poor reputation. Indeed, rites may be or may, over time, become pretentious and inauthentic. But we would not want to establish a theoretical approach to ritual in which the integrity or sincerity of people engaged in ritual is implicitly doubted. If we are to use the words "perform" and "act" in studying ritual, we need to realize these connote more than merely something for "show," and Schechner deals with this problem through the notion of "efficacy."

There are similarities between games, play, theater, and ritual—they are all examples of "performance;" but there are differences too. Schechner places performance on a continuum that runs from *efficacy* to *entertainment*. This move is made to avoid imagining ritual and theater as oppositional categories. Nō theater and the kōan tradition are not opposites but rather interrelated cultural forms. Ritual can entertain, and theater can have real consequences. Nevertheless, like other theorists, Schechner tends to associate ritual with efficacy. The more theater pushes in the direction of efficacy and transformation, the more ritual-like it becomes; the more ritual heads in the direction of entertainment, the more theatrical-like (and the more entertaining) it becomes. When a performance is efficacious, Schechner speaks of "transformance," a coinage meant to emphasize the role of performance (whether ritual or dramatic) in processes of social, psychological, or spiritual transformation.

Schechner is particularly interested in cultural forms where entertainment and efficacy come to form a tight braid, as in the cases of Greek tragedy, the medieval mystery plays sponsored by the Catholic church, and Elizabethan theater. Aristotle introduced the notion of catharsis in his discussion of tragedy. Through tragedy, he writes, the "emotions that strongly affect some souls" can be given "pleasurable relief" and they "calm down as if they had been medically treated and purged (katharseos)." Tragedy was performed in Athens as part of the annual Festival of Dionysus; it introduced the element of spectatorship into ritual contexts, but involved more than mere entertainment. The mix of entertainment and efficacy in Greek tragedy is one reason for the origins debate in ritual studies: Did ritual become theater, or theater ritual? Schechner bypasses such debates by inquiring about efficacy. The healing potential of theatrical performance has long been recognized. That performance can be an especially powerful means for triggering the release of feeling and emotion explains the fusion of psychotherapy and performance in drama, music, and dance therapies. The use of theater and performance for purposes of healing is increasingly common in war-torn areas and in community development and reconciliation projects.

Schechner's efficacy-entertainment dyad is partly a descriptive tool, but it has a normative dimension as well. The best ritual (or theater, for that matter) will weave together the qualities of entertainment and efficacy. If ritual becomes overly prescriptive, staid, and dutiful, too much like work, it is unlikely to be experienced as joyous or entertaining; should theater aim too far in the direction of making a practical difference, it may become pretentious and the seats are likely to be empty. On the other hand, if ritual is doing no transformative work but is merely a way to pleasantly pass the time in the comfortable presence of like-minded others, it lacks gravitas and, in time, will likely wither.

Embodiment and inscription

"Embodiment" is a tricky term in ritual studies. In part, the word points a more integrative understanding of mind and body. Some cognitive scientists refer to the "embodied mind," a coinage that attempts to overcome the long-standing Cartesian mind-body dualism in the Western intellectual tradition. In ritual studies, the notion of embodiment has a couple of distinct connotations. The term can refer, in a rather suspicious fashion, to the ways in which ideas and values are inscribed into the body through ritual practice. Second, the language of embodiment highlights the fact that ritual is one of the ways people go about making sense of their world. Like reason, ritual is a way of knowing.

The notion of inscription is closely associated with the thought of Catherine Bell, who, in the tradition of Pierre Bourdieu, takes a rather suspicious view of ritual. For Bell, ritual is mainly about the production of "ritualized" bodies. Ritualists are imagined as a kind of malleable wax, into which ritual impresses values, beliefs, and social roles and statuses. Bell refers to the ritualized body as containing "socially instinctive automatisms," suggesting that the body engaging in ritual is not really engaging at all but is more of a passive receptor of codes and scripts that lie outside, in our wider social world. The language of "inscription" and "automatisms" removes agency from ritual actors, placing it in ritualized practices. Bell further suggests that those engaged in ritual fundamentally "misrecognize" what they are doing. Gift-giving, for example, seems an act of generosity; what we are really doing, however, is establishing a tacit relationship of power in which the recipient becomes indebted to the gift-giver. If we were to recognize what was really happening, the function of gift-giving (establishing lines of authority and dominance) would implode, hence Bell's basic assumption that ritual necessarily proceeds on the basis of misrecognition and "false consciousness." A classic example of ritual "inscription" is Davis-Floyd's interpretation of Western hospital birth, which reinforces dominant values and beliefs (technocracy, efficiency, and a distrust of instincts and the body) on the bodies and minds of its members. Certainly there are cases in which ritual actors are largely blind and passive to the implications of the rites in which they participate; studying the exploitive and ideological dimensions of ritual is important. But embodiment can mean more than rendering people susceptible to hegemonic values and beliefs.

A second meaning of embodiment in ritual studies, quite different from that found in "practice theory," emphasizes that the body and senses are noetic channels in their own right. In the opening scene of the acclaimed film *The Sacrifice*, written and directed by Andrei Tarkovsky, Alexander, an aging professor and theater critic, his young son in tow, wanders a bleak shoreline, plants a scraggly tree, and ponders the mysteries of life. Alexander tells his son a short tale of a monk who each day carries a dipper of water up a mountain to water a tree. He does this for three years, and one morning, he arrives to find the tree in full blossom. Alexander continues: "You know, sometimes I say to myself, if every single day, at exactly the same stroke of the clock one were to perform the same act, like a ritual, unchanging, systematic, every day at the same time, the world would be changed. Yes, something would change, it would have to." A question posed in this scene is whether a ritual act has efficacy and power, whether, in the face of existential angst and meaninglessness, it is easier to act oneself into a new way of thinking than think oneself into a new way of acting. As Alexander suggests, there is surely a relationship between our doings and our experience, between action and thought.

In philosophy, epistemology is the study of how we come to know what we know. In the wake of the scientific revolution and the Enlightenment, Western culture has come to privilege reason as the chief and best means of acquiring knowledge. The Enlightenment tradition of reason has not only separated fact and value but also mind and body. René Descartes, in his effort to arrive at sure and clear knowledge, found it necessary to eliminate the sensual body; as he famously wrote, "my essence consists only in my being a thinking thing." Such an epistemology does not bode well for ritual. Ritual is first and foremost a doing, something done with the body; and if the body is an obstacle to knowledge, so too is ritual. Among the various cultural factors leading to diminution and demeaning of ritual in the modern West has been the epistemological privileging of reason, over and against the body. In the context of the modern university, in teaching, for example, I cannot ask students to dance, or to pray, or to meditate, or to ingest peyote, or even to, upon entering the classroom, remove their shoes. In fact, if I were to do so, such ritualizations would lead, so the suspicion goes, to something the precise opposite of knowledge. But clearly, as the scene in Tarkovsky's film suggests, how we comport our body has ripple effects in our understanding and relationship to the world. Ritual, a formalized, stylized, and repetitive handling of the body, is also a way of knowing.

Michel Foucault makes a distinction between philosophy and spirituality. Philosophy, he says, attempts to articulate the conditions and limits that circumscribe a subject's access to truth. Spirituality, in contrast, consists in a set of practices through which "the subject carries out the necessary transformations on himself in order to have access to the truth." Embedded in the word "spirituality" is, of course, the word "ritual." Ritual knowledge, the knowledge gained from spiritual practices, postulates that in order to know there must be a transformation of the subject. Foucault emphasizes that in the philosophical traditions of antiquity, philosophy and spirituality were bedfellows. The question of how to have access to the truth and ritual as a transformative practice allowing access to the truth were not separated. The philosophical schools of antiquity were highly ritualized affairs, the various elements and practices of which Foucault develops under the rubric of "care of the self."

The experience and expression of going on a sacred journey crosses cultures, religions, and territories. The human need to leave home, travel to a sacred place in order to establish ties with sacred beings, gain physical and spiritual healing, and receive new knowledge so that life can be renewed is a fundamental dimension of religious life. Pilgrimage to sacred sites (places of apparitions, birthplaces, tombs, caves, mountains, relic sites), though sometimes carried out in opposition to theological and ecclesiastical

6. Two pilgrims dressed in traditional *hakui* (white robe) and *henro* (conical-shaped hat) carry the *kongōtsue* (walking stick) and enter the precincts of one of eighty-eight temples on the Shikoku pilgrimage trail.

authorities, is a persistent manifestation of all religions throughout history. The classical, prototypical pilgrimage sites include: Jerusalem (Jewish, Christian, and Muslim); Rome (Christian); Mecca (Muslim); Mount Wu-t'ai, China (Buddhist); Benares, Indian (Hindu); and Mt. Kalish (Tibetan). In addition to these major, global centers, there are thousands of other local and regional pilgrimage sites found all over the world and spread throughout religious traditions. Typologically, pilgrimage is sometimes considered a rite of mobility, along with parades and processions, quests, and the more mundane rites of greeting and exiting.

The contemporary study of pilgrimage reveals great diversity. Included in pilgrimage studies are not only the classical sites but also postmodern places such as Disneyland, secular locales such as battlefields and disaster sites, heritage homes, and the graves of popular musicians. Pilgrimage is a field of study where the sacred and secular mingle and intertwine. Owing to this diversity, a straightforward, broadly accepted definition of pilgrimage is difficult to find. Sometimes with my students, we brainstorm features or characteristics of pilgrimage, in the effort to understand the difficulties involved in creating definitions. Students quickly identify several criteria as constitutive of pilgrimage, and then the debate and discussion begins:

1. Destination: The location must be "sacred." (Is Disney a pilgrimage site?)

2. Distance: The journey must take one across some sort of physical or cultural border. (Can one pilgrimage without leaving familiar ground?)

3. Magnitude: There must be a collective dimension. (Can one pilgrimage alone?)

4. Motivation: The motivation must be religious. (Is a visit to the Pearl Harbor memorial religious?)

Based on these criteria, we typically arrive at a definition such as this: pilgrimage is a prolonged event, involving travel away from local territory, undertaken by many people, to a sacred place, as an act of devotion, informed by religious motives. The terms in the definition beg, of course, many questions. Eventually, another element enters into the discussion: to count as pilgrimage there must be significant ardor and difficulty, especially physical difficulty; the journey is taxing on the body, even potentially dangerous.

Historically, risk, danger, and exertion have been central features of pilgrimage. When someone left a parish in medieval England for Jerusalem, there was possibility they might not return; the roads were dangerous, the journey long. To this day, some Tibetan Buddhists practice pilgrimage in India, Nepal, and Tibet via prostrations. The pilgrim performs a full prostration to the ground, with the body fully extended, arms stretched out in front

7. A Buddhist pilgrim performs a full prostration during his journey to Lhasa, Tibet. Traditionally, pilgrimage has been a physically rigorous, even dangerous experience.

of the head; they get up, take three-and-a-half steps forward, and perform another prostration. Such pilgrimages can last months, even years, depending on the destination. Food is simple, the conditions and terrain often harsh.

To consider ritual as an alternative, secondary medium for expressing what could otherwise be (perhaps more easily) expressed is to miss what is distinctive about ritual: a rite requires doing—if it is not performed, there is no rite. The manner of the performance is important. We can learn through the use of our body; knowledge is corporeal (in contrast to cerebral), active (not simply contemplative), and potentially transformative (not merely speculative).

Levi-Strauss's shaman

Claude Levi-Strauss is one of the founding figures of structuralism. Generally, structuralism and performance theory are at odds with one another. In his widely read essay, "The Sorcerer and His Magic," published in 1949, based in part on his fieldwork in Brazil, Levi-Strauss touches on a key issue in performance approaches to ritual. Levi-Strauss does not deny the physiological efficacy of certain magical practices, their ability to act on what he calls the "sympathetic nervous system," but the full "efficacy of magic," he writes, "implies a belief in magic"—that is, magic and shamanism are psychological phenomena. A few pages later, we stumble across an odd paragraph—odd because it seems important, seems to reframe the general thread of both his approach and argument, and odd because Levi-Strauss drops the matter as quickly as he takes it up:

> In treating his patient the shaman also offers his audience a performance. What is this performance? Risking a rash generalization on the basis of a few observations, we shall say that it always involves the shaman's enactment of the "call," or the initial crisis which brought him the revelation of his condition. But we must not be deceived by the word performance. The shaman does not limit himself to reproducing or miming certain events. He actually relives them in all their vividness, originality, and violence.

"We must not be deceived by the word performance." Here, Levi-Strauss warns the reader not to gloss performance as mere performance, as secondary to mental processes. There is a power in the performance, and to ignore it, Levi-Strauss implicitly warns, is to ignore something crucial to how shamanism works. This paragraph, oddly enough, undercuts the representational approach to ritual characteristic of structuralism. Also: the shaman "actually relives" his call. What does it mean to "actually relive" something, as opposed to simply reliving it? Why the "actually," if not to press home the ontological reality of the performance? On the verge of a full-blown performance approach to his topic, Levi-Strauss pulls back to compare the shaman's work with that of the psychoanalyst.

Like a compressed spring, turn a rite loose, let it uncoil, and it can do work. Why? Ritual performance, ritual enactment has power. Victor Turner introduced the idea of "performing ethnography" into research and teaching. Turner would have students enact ritual scenes or scripts brought home from the field. The practice was and remains controversial. The question informing it, however, is pressing: Can we have access to knowledge, understanding, even truth, if nothing is demanded of us by way of changing or altering our being as a subject? A Hopi kachina initiation and a Tibetan pilgrimage make this kind of transformative change in the subject, affected through ritual participation, the condition upon which knowledge is premised.

Many theorists of ritual who use a performance approach ask us to consider the noetic implications of ritual action. Do initiation rites, for example, have more than symbolic or declarative power? Might dancing and drumming for days on end during an initiation rite induce a cognitive shift that so alters our perception of the world that the moment of the dance does not merely formally mark a new and collectively agreed upon social status, but also effects a break with a previous way of being? Could it be that our ideas, values, attitudes are not the antecedents of action but rather constituted by means of performance? For Schechner, in good acting, "the doing of the action of a feeling is enough to arouse the feeling both in the doer and in the receiver," an observation similar to that of Zeami mentioned earlier. Feelings and ideas are not simply absorbed through consciousness but formed, given body through enactment.

Chapter 7
The fortunes of ritual

The *Liji*, known in English as the *Book of Rites,* is one of five texts forming the canon of early Confucian literature. These texts, compiled and edited around the second century BCE, provide insight into the religious and moral character and debates of early China. Among the contents of the *Liji* is a social cosmology, describing a fall from a state of harmony and well-being, the period of the "Grand Unity" when the "Great Way" pervaded the world, to a state of self-centeredness, discord, and thievery. The *Liji* further tells of the appearance of "profound persons" who offered the means by which to re-establish and maintain a modicum of unity and order. Chief among these means to counter humanity's fallen state are devices, guides, practices, called *li*, a term most frequently translated as "rituals" or "ceremonies." *Li* are imagined as knots, binding society together; in the absence of these ritual knots, society would be formless and individuals disconnected from one another. Cut off from a natural goodness and harmony, we can only devise, regulate, and maintain "Modest Prosperity" through ritual action. Ritual is a device and technique for generating and maintaining order, good will, and a sense of belonging.

Anticipating Durkheim by more than two millennia, the *Liji* claims that ritual has the capacity to organize otherwise atomized individuals into a cohesive group. Ritual gets everyone on the team pulling in the same direction, as it were, but is no guarantee of harmony. Ritual practice may go awry, or traditional rites may not be up to dealing with social and cultural changes. Yet ritual is all we have, hence the profound concern in the *Liji* to both argue the merits of ritual and to understand and explain the conditions under which ritual fails to function as a substitute for the "Great Way." Fast-forward two thousand years and halfway around the globe to Enlightenment Europe, and we find a very different attitude toward ritual.

The philosopher Charles Taylor refers to a "social imaginary" as the way a society imagines and practices social life. The social imaginary depicted in Confucian texts such as the *Liji* reserves a prominent place for ritual and ceremony; the social imaginary of the modern West is very different. Our modern social imaginary is the product of a multitude of interlocking changes (technological, economic, religious, political) that comprise the modern world; one feature of it is a decline in the esteem and presence of ritual. In his study of the modern world as a "secular age," Taylor refers to a process of "excarnation," the "transfer of our religious life out of bodily forms of ritual, worship, practice, so that it [religion] comes more and more to reside 'in the head.'"

The philosophes of the Enlightenment promoted individual autonomy, rationality, and social reform; they also took aim at both religious beliefs and ritual. Ritual came to be viewed as staid and outmoded, a superstitious remnant of a primitive past, a past that prevented humanity from truly advancing. Ritual, like its cousin myth, became a matter of suspicion and derision. The word "myth" was yoked to falsehood—a myth was a lie, an untruth, at best, a fanciful story—while ritual was derided as habitual, obsessive, fetishized behavior—antiquated, boring, ineffectual, and repressive. Ritual's reputation in the modern, secularizing West was sullied, its practice ghettoized. Such overly suspicious and negative conceptions of ritual remain part of the intellectual and cultural milieu in Europe and North America.

Ritualism and primitivism

In the wake of the Reformation, there began a process of
de-ritualization across Western Europe, a curtailing of ritual that
continued through the Enlightenment and Industrial Revolution.
As scholars in the nineteenth and early twentieth centuries began
studying societies at the edges of the modern, industrial West,
ritual was conspicuous by its presence. Ritual was also a central
feature of the textual traditions of antiquity, to which scholarship
was increasingly focusing attention, using the new historical
and comparative methods. In both anthropological and textual
research, developing theory pointed to rites, especially rites
associated with sacrifice and magic, as markers of difference
between "primitive" and "modern" societies. Influential thinkers
found in ritual evidence in support of theories of cultural
evolution. Societies advance, so the claim went, in three stages,
from magic to religion to science. In the ethological view, ritual
is a kind of collective social instinct; this meant that those
societies strongly governed by complex and pervasive ritual
systems—typically, non-Western cultures, peoples on the
margins of modern, industrial, technological society—are
more "instinctual," and thus further removed from the rational,
technological, individualist, liberal, enlightened culture of
modern Europe. Suspicion of ritual among intellectual and
political elites seemed natural enough, since ritual was perceived
as a sign of cultural backwardness.

A discourse of primitivism and racism is part of the history of
ritual theory. It is common in early studies of ritual to encounter
pejorative conceptions of ritual, typically through the notion of
"ritualism." Listen to the language of the poet, literary critic, and
anthropologist Andrew Lang, in his comprehensive *Myth, Ritual
and Religion,* published in 1887. Surveying the development of
religion in India, Lang comments how over "the whole mass of
ancient [Vedic] mythology the new mythology of a debased
Brahmanic ritualism grew like some luxurious and baneful

parasite." Vedic myth, we learn, is "originally derived from nature worship," and in "an infinite majority of cases only reflects natural phenomena through a veil of ritualistic corruptions." Lang's language reveals the broad-based contours of the intellectual landscape of his day. We like to think, perhaps, we are well past such stereotypes and prejudices, but the sediments of culture are slow to shift. Ritual is still commonly associated with "ritualism" and the "ritualistic"—neither of which connotes much of value. The panic twenty years ago over cases of "satanic ritual abuse" and more recent discussions of genital "mutilation" give evidence to how the imagination of ritual in Western cultures continues to be informed by primitivist stereotypes.

As the fields of anthropology, sociology, and history of religions consolidated in the early decades of the twentieth century, ritual was given some credibility via the Durkhemian tradition of social functionalism. Religious practices were seen as vehicles of social order and stability, and hence of a certain value; the problem, however, was that ritual functioned in a rather unconscious fashion. Ritual may work so far as it goes, it just does not go very far; ritual occludes a rational understanding of natural, social, and psychological processes and dynamics. Participants engage in ritual, the argument went, without really knowing what they are doing; ritual was a veil masking reality. The slow march of Enlightenment meant giving up irrational and repressive group rites for an emancipated reason and individual autonomy. The important point here is that early theories of ritual were yoked to an evolutionary perspective, which was often little more than a thinly veiled expression of cultural superiority. The pejorative language and images of "ritualism" and "ritualistic" entered the vocabulary and worldview of the modern West.

Freud, for example, described the obsessional neuroses he encountered in his patients as akin to religious rites and practices, thereby framing religion as a collective obsessional neurosis: ritual equals pathology. The repetitive, rhythmic, and formalized behavior of obsessive actions, Freud suggested, are the result of repression and rooted in fear and guilt; obsessive acts are signals of what is really going on, beneath the surface, even though patients are completely unaware of the real meaning of their behavior. Similarly, the motives and meanings of religious ritual are unknown to participants, who are merely going through the motions, performing "ritualistic" behaviors and gestures the significance of which they do not understand. For Freud, religious beliefs and practices could be an understandable source of consolation, but this good feeling was bought at the high price of being unconscious.

If the psychoanalytic tradition has been generally wary of ritual, associating it with "primitive" societies and psychologies, we find similar sentiments in sociology, too. The influential sociologist Robert Merton, writing in the middle decades of the twentieth century, conceived ritual as a form of social deviance, a way of adapting to social "anomie." All societies, suggested Merton, are characterized by anomie, conceived as gap or distance between collective idealized goals and the individual's ability to realize these goals. For those who cannot make the grade, there are forms of "deviant adaptation," including criminal activity (where one breaks rules and laws to attain socially prized goals), "retreatism" (where one withdraws from the game into alcoholism and drug addiction), and "ritualism" (where one holds firm to social scripts and forms, while resigning oneself to the fact that social accomplishment is forever beyond one's reach). Ritual is thus grouped with crime and addiction (not the best of company), and imagined as infused with a spirit of defeatism and resignation. In Merton's hands, ritual was once again reduced to "ritualism," the performance of mere externalities without any authentic commitment or depth of feeling for the values and ideas embedded and projected in rites and ceremonies. Ritual as ritualism is sham.

These broadly negative conceptions of ritual that developed in the modern West were not driven solely by scholarship. In the second half of the nineteenth century, elements within the Church of England began an aggressive campaign to promote and reform the liturgy. Many of the changes—vesting in colorful robes, celebrating the Eucharist facing east, adding processions to the liturgy and iconography to churches—met with fierce resistance and debate. Part of the issue was long-standing tensions between Catholics and Protestants in Britain; but also at play were culturally pervasive negative attitudes toward ritual. Highly stylized, formalized ritual was seen as a theatrical, upper-class affair, filled with pretence and hypocrisy. Some critics charged that the changes wrought to the liturgy were making men more "effeminate." Britain's prime minister Benjamin Disraeli referred to the ritualist movement as a "mass in a masquerade." The ritualists were severely attacked as a threat to English identity and the moral fabric of English society. The controversy led to parliament passing a Public Worship Regulation Act in 1874; under the act, many clergy were charged and prosecuted. Ritual was not only "primitive," it was illegal.

Loss and longing

Another way to understand and experience the relative absence of ritual in modern Western culture is not as an advance forward but as a step backward, not as a gain but as a loss. If many intellectuals through the late nineteenth and twentieth centuries developed a suspicious view of ritual, looking forward to the day of ritual's last rites, others were reflecting on the great "excarnation" in analyses characterized by ambivalence and nostalgia. Durkheim may have been studying the rites and ceremonies of others, but he was doing so, in part, to better understand his own place and time. Durkheim perceived a connection between social anomie in modernity (the fragmentation of shared, collective identity and the weakening of social institutions) and the shrinking fortunes of ritual in the West. Similarly, Julian Huxley applied his ethological findings to reflection on the contemporary state of ritual. Huxley saw a causal connection between the ills of the twentieth century (lack of social bonding, poor communication, escalation of conflict, mass killing in protracted wars) and ineffectual ritualization in society. Huxley reasoned that since ritualization is socially functional—regulating everything from mating to war—then a society that does not tend to patterns of ritualization is playing with fire.

Mary Douglas, in her book *Natural Symbols* (1970), opened with a chapter titled "Away from Ritual," in which she discussed both the modern West's suspicious withdrawal from the world of ritual and the prevalent, negative conceptions of ritual found in sociological theory. Rejection of ritual is, for Douglas, the rejection of public forms of solidarity and institution building, and hence a failure of nerve in the heady days of the 1960s counterculture. Douglas further argued that the deprecatory use of the word "ritual" in the theory of her day was unacceptable, and she developed a more neutral conception in terms of symbolic communication.

Perhaps the most ambitious and influential scholarly effort to re-orient attitudes toward ritual came through the work of the comparative historian of religion Mircea Eliade. Religion, for Eliade, is a question of orientation and centeredness, a posture toward and experience of the world created in part through ritual, in particular through initiation. Initiation, he claimed, is the fundamental means by which people become human and the cosmos made sacred. Eliade opened his classic 1958 text on initiation by framing the plight of "modern man" as that of living in a "desacralized cosmos," and linked this state of affairs to the "disappearance of meaningful rites of passage." If one agrees with Eliade that "initiation lies at the core of any genuine human life," then a society without meaningful initiatory practices can only be inauthentic and shallow. Eliade conceived a society's principal rites as a means of renewal. Social energies necessarily flag and falter; for this reason, ritual reconnects participants with the original energies and actors "in the beginning." The initiate ritually "dies" to an old state, enters the womb of renewal and transformation, and returns to the world reborn and remade.

As with scholarly theory, ritual on the ground was also receiving more appreciative attention. Through the latter half of the nineteenth century, we detect a return to ritual within currents of religious life in Europe and North America; the ritualists in the Church of England are an obvious example. John Ruskin, best known for his work as painter, encouraged Protestant architecture in England to adopt gothic forms, cautiously encouraging a revitalization of liturgy. Ruskin also lent his support to the revival of folk customs such as maypole dancing, which had been largely suppressed since the days of the Reformation. Protestant American culture was similarly responding to ritual deprivation. Many evangelical Protestants embraced an embodied and dramatized style of liturgy. Ritual interests and experimentation in nineteenth-century Anglo-American culture informed the rise of revivalist camp-meeting movements, as well as the burgeoning interest in spiritualism.

Through the twentieth century the idea of ritual impoverishment develops: one of the ills of Western culture is the absence of ritual, and the recovery of ritual is a cure to what ails us. In the wake of Eliade, a good deal of the theorizing of initiation includes the claim that in industrial, modern, secular society, passage rites associated with birth and initiation have either disappeared entirely or are no longer effective; where passage rites are a going concern (weddings and funerals), commoditization and packaging has run roughshod over authenticity and efficacy. There is a strong stream of ritual theory that makes connection between a (supposed) pervasive spiritual and social anomie in Western culture and a lack of initiation rites to guide and move young people into adulthood. This assumption has generated a good deal of *ritualizing*, a term introduced by Ronald Grimes to distinguish formal and traditionally accepted rites from the practice of deliberately cultivating new ones. In Western societies, the call for recovery and reinvention of rites of passage has been strongly directed at initiation, in particular male initiation. In the absence of passage rites it is not uncommon that major transitions or stages in the life cycle become ritualized. In the case of adolescent males, unsupervised, spontaneous, and often violent ad hoc initiation practices are common.

Ritual longing and active ritualizing are not without potential problems. Invented initiation rites in the modern Western world rely on a good deal of ritual "borrowing" from other cultures. The Eliadean assumption that the ritual practices of "traditional" societies are fecund tools for the revitalization of modern, industrial society has idealized those practices and created a hunger for them; this hunger has encouraged ritual appropriation. Many North Americans of European descent have turned to the initiation rites of Native traditions for their spiritual goods: sweat lodges, vision quests, sacred pipes, rattles, and spirit catchers make up the bill of fare of many workshops and retreats. But for many Native people, non-Native fascination with Native religious, symbolic, and ritual systems represents the ongoing colonization of Native North Americans. The appropriation debate first focused on issues of land claims and the return of artifacts and human remains but has widened to include ritual practices. Ritual syncretism is pervasive throughout history and across cultures. But if we are to engage in ritualizing, we need to be aware of the political and moral debate around borrowing (or should we say "stealing"?) the ritual traditions of others.

Ritual and public life

Recent ritual theory has witnessed a revival of earlier efforts to articulate the relationship between ritual and group solidarity. The French intellectual Alexis de Tocqueville, writing about mid-nineteenth-century America, coined the term "individualism" to describe the emerging "American character" in a social context of a growing market economy, an emphasis on personal autonomy

and equality, and democratic government. Tocqueville described
the phenomenon of individualism:

> Each person, withdrawn into himself, behaves as though he is a
> stranger to the destiny of all the others. His children and his good
> friends constitute for him the whole of the human species. As for
> his transactions with his fellow citizens, he may mix among them,
> but he sees them not; he touches them, but he does not feel them;
> he exists only in himself and for himself alone. And if on these
> terms there remains in his mind a sense of family, there no longer
> remains a sense of society.

A similar dynamic was detected in Europe, exemplified in the
thought of the German sociologist Georg Simmel. Society, argued
Simmel, writing at the turn of the twentieth century, was becoming
less sociable, less convivial. He wrote of an inherent drive to
associate, to transcend the individual ego through union with
others, a need that had been frustrated by the evacuation of public
forms of culture, such as collective ritual. "The vitality of real
individuals, in their sensitivities and attractions, in the fullness of
their impulses and convictions...shows itself in the flow of a lightly
amusing play." Playfulness and the freedom to play are necessary to
the kind of union that interested Simmel, precisely the ethos that
accompanied the long tradition of carnival and local festivals in
Europe, ritual forms that were suppressed or ignored in the course
of the Reformation, the Enlightenment, the period of absolutism,
and the rise of fascism and communism in Europe.

A central feature of the "modern social imaginary" is the decline
of embodied, public life, what Richard Sennett refers to as *The
Fall of Public Man* and Charles Taylor as the great "excarnation."
In *Ritual and Consequences,* Adam Seligman and his colleagues
contrast historical changes to modern society in terms of the
categories of "sincerity" and "ritual." Modern life, they argue,
is premised on sincerity, an inward-looking, individualistic effort
to grasp the unvarnished truth; ritual, in contrast, is a centrifugal,

collective, and inherently subjunctive space that encourages sociability and communal values. Though their typology is somewhat polemical—ritual can be strongly indicative, even oppressive—they do raise a question that many are beginning to pursue: What are the consequences for a society that devalues the collective experiences found in and through ritual?

Richard Sennett, in *Together: The Rituals, Pleasures and Politics of Cooperation*, published in 2012, argues that our rituals of citizenship and sociability have been turned into spectacles, with participants reduced to mere observers and consumers. The problem Sennett detects—the pervasive erosion of our ability to cooperate in the modern world—is met with an answer that draws upon a Ruskin-like embrace of artisan-like collectives held together, in large measure, by the intricate daily round of ritualizations that breed manners, civility, dialogue, and care for one another. Pie-in-the-sky nostalgia? Perhaps. Yet the role of ritual in matters of deference and demeanor, so detailed by Erving Goffman, likely has something to say to a society seemingly incapable of the most basic forms of civility.

Another dimension of the return of ritual is found in the recent growth of festivals across much of Europe and, to a lesser degree, in North America. In the past generation, public festivals and celebration have been renewed and re-invented on a vast, perhaps unprecedented, scale. Festive celebration involves a periodic gathering of a group, in a marked-off space and time for the purposes of play, engaging in aesthetic activity, sharing food, exchanging gifts, stories, songs, and then dispersal. Such moments of common action and feeling "both wrench us out of the everyday, and seem to put us in touch with something exceptional, beyond ourselves." Charles Taylor, whom I am quoting here, calls this the category of the "festive," and it is inherently related to the development of a more immediate, active, face-to face public sphere. It is also, suggests Taylor, "among the new forms of religion in our world."

Linking public ritual with sociability points beyond the typical sociological emphasis on social structure toward matters of individual and group expression, performance, and play. One could argue, of course, that sociable behavior maintains the solidarities and hierarchies of a group. But we could just as well argue that festive celebration is fundamental to human being, and that in the absence of periodic festive gathering, social values and solidarity are likely to falter. The festive social is irrepressible, indestructible, which is to say, fundamental, bedrock, a foundation of social life. So it is no surprise, after several centuries of relative success by church and state at suppressing public festivals, festive culture is experiencing a renaissance in the streets and squares of Europe—as, for example, in Wittenberg, Germany, the historical seat of the Reformation.

Festival (or celebration) is a ritual type, found across cultures. One of the characteristics of festival is that festivalgoers are part of the production; this active participation is quite unlike, say, proscenium theater, where an audience-performer boundary is demarcated and maintained throughout the performance. In the enactment of a festival, spectators and consumers are encouraged to become performers and producers. A festival succeeds or fails on the willingness of the audience to engage in festive behavior. The degree of separation between performers and audience is one feature often used to distinguish ritual from theater. Where a high degree of separation exists, we have formal theater; at the other end of the continuum, where spectator becomes participant, is ritual. Play is also characterized by the absence of a performer-audience boundary: if you are watching, you are not playing. Festivals that move in the direction of audience participation head in the direction of ritual and play, and those attending the event also play a part in its production: where the audience is passive, though, we have a cultural performance, looked upon and consumed by spectators.

A festival is about as sociable an occasion as one can imagine, precisely because one can disappear in the crowd. A festivalgoer engages with, interacts with, one's fellow citizens; a festival, on the whole, gathers people together, not on the level of personal intimacy and acquaintance but community and sociability. Play and jest are the paradigmatic gestures of festivals. The contemporary revival of local festivals sanctions role playing, allowing for diverse performances, creating an occasion during which citizens can present themselves and their doings to one another on a public stage.

One of the defining characteristics of a "spectacle" is the presence of a sharp distinction between audience and performers. In a spectacle, actors perform, while spectators watch, at a distance. In festival, in contrast, everyone is called to celebrate together. To name an event as a "spectacle" is to introduce a certain suspicion or criticism. A festival is different. Rather than generating a sense of diffuse awe and wonder, emotions that captivate while distancing the spectator from the action (think of gladiatorial games), festivals are joyous occasions or are meant to be so. The French sociologist Guy Debord argued that modernity is a "society of the spectacle," which is to say "an epoch without festivals." The distinction here is between the production of spectacle by elites for nationalist, consumptive, and commercial purposes versus a more organic, cyclical domain of festivity that emerges from a people's productive labor. Annual festivals become embedded in the sociocultural life of the city and region in which they take place; they are repeated, worked on, anticipated year after year.

Festivals are often thought of as events or cultural, but they are also social institutions and, in the language of the social critic Ivan Illich, they are "tools." "Tools," writes Illich, "are intrinsic to social relationships. An individual relates himself in action to his society through the use of tools that he actively masters .... To the degree that he masters his tools, he can invest the world with his meaning; to the degree that he is mastered by his tools, the shape of the tool determines his own self-image." Illich's definition of a convivial tool or institution is precise: "Convivial tools are those

8. **Masked figures processing in the Velvet Carnival, Prague. Inaugurated in 2012, this procession aims to keep alive the spirit of progressive social action associated with the peaceful Velvet Revolution, which marked the end of communism in Czechoslovakia.**

ones which give each person who uses them the greatest opportunity to enrich the environment with the fruits of his or her vision."

Many contemporary festivals embody this convivial ethos, promoting broad participation and encouraging self-expression; in so doing they "enrich the environment." The "invention of tradition" school, exemplified in the work of Eric Hobsbawm and David Kertzer, has greatly influenced the study of public ritual. Both scholars focus on political ceremony and conceive ritual as a tool for creating ideology and maintaining hegemonic power. To be sure, ritual may serve such ends, but not necessarily so. There are different kinds of ritual tools. Many contemporary festivals are turning away from the indicative, didactic, monologic, spectacle-like ceremony of the era of state nationalism toward a festive mood, characterized by broad participation, diversity, spontaneity, and improvisation. Ritual may acquire strength by virtue of being a hallowed, time honored, ancestral practice. But it may also be embraced because it is effective at achieving certain goals, or simply because it is enjoyable. Festivals and public celebration have been and continue to be important tools in the creation of sociability and conviviality for a culture desperately in need of a revived public sphere.

References

Chapter 1

Tom Driver, *Liberating Rites: Understanding the Transformative Power of Ritual* (Boulder, CO: Westview, 1998), 36–37.

Tom Driver, Werner Binder, and Barry Stephenson, "What's at Stake in Torture," in *Ritual, Media, and Conflict*, ed. Ronald L. Grimes et al., 235–36 (New York: Oxford University Press, 2011).

Gwynne Dyer, *War* (New York: Dorsey, 1985), 6.

Adam Hoebel, "Law-Ways of the Primitive Eskimos," *Journal of Criminal Law and Criminology* 31, no. 6 (1941): 663–83.

Julian Huxley, introduction to "A Discussion on Ritualization of Behaviour in Animals and Man," *Philosophical Transactions of the Royal Society of London*, Series B 251 (1966): 249–71.

F. B. Kirkman, quoted in Richard Burkhardt Jr., *Patterns of Behavior: Konrad Lozenz, Niko Tinbergen, and the Founding of Ethology* (Chicago: University of Chicago Press, 2005), 100.

E. O. Wilson, *Sociobiology: The New Synthesis* (Cambridge, MA: Harvard University Press, 1975), 247.

Chapter 2

Richard Bradley, *Ritual and Domestic Life in Prehistoric Europe* (London: Routledge, 2005).

Walter Burkert, *Structure and History in Greek Mythology and Ritual* (Berkeley: University of California Press, 1979), 91.

James Frazer, *The Golden Bough: A Study in Magic and Religion* (New York: Cosimo, 2009 [1922]), 337, 388, 324.

Rene Girard, *Violence and the Sacred* (Baltimore, MD: Johns Hopkins University Press, 1972), 306.

Ronald L. Grimes, *Rite out of Place* (New York: Oxford University Press, 2006), 109.

Werner Herzog (director), *Cave of Forgotten Dreams* (Kinosmith Films, 2011).

Homer, *The Iliad*, trans. Robert Fagels (New York: Penguin, 1990), 92–93.

J. D. Lewis-Williams, "Harnessing the Brain: Vision and Shamanism in Upper Paleolithic Western Europe," in *Beyond Art: Pleistocene Image and Symbol*, ed. Margaret Conkey, 326 (Berkeley: University of California Press 1997).

Klaus Schmidt, "Gobekli Tepe, Southeastern Turkey: A Preliminary Report on the 1995–1999 Excavations," *Paleorient* 26, no. 1 (2001): 46.

Jonathan Z. Smith, "The Bare Facts of Ritual," *History of Religions* 20, nos. 1–2 (1980): 125.

Walter A. Van Beek, *The Dancing Dead: Ritual and Religion Among the Kapsiki/Higi of North Cameroon and Northeastern Nigeria* (New York: Oxford University Press, 2012), 97–98.

Ritual

Chapter 3

Emile Durkheim, *The Elementary Forms of Religious Life*, trans. Karen E. Fields (New York: Free Press, 1995), 212, 217, 314.

Clifford Geertz, *Local Knowledge* (New York: Basic Books, 2000), 125.

Max Gluckman, *Politics, Law and Ritual in Tribal Societies* (Chicago: Aldine, 1965), 164–65.

Eric Hobsbawm and T. O Ranger, eds., *The Invention of Tradition* (New York: Cambridge University Press, 1983), 2.

Edward Muir, *Civic Ritual in Renaissance Venice* (Princeton, NJ: Princeton University Press, 1981), 302.

Roy Rappaport, *Ritual and Religion in the Making of Humanity* (New York: Cambridge University Press, 1999), 8, 1–3, 24.

Victor Turner, "Are There Universals of Performance in Myth, Ritual and Drama?" in *By Means of Performance: Intercultural Studies of Theatre and Ritual*, ed. Richard Schechner and Willa Apel, 12–13 (New York: Cambridge University Press, 1991).

Chapter 4

Vincent Crapanzano, "Rite of Return: Circumcision in Morocco," in *The Psychoanalytic Study of Society* 9, ed. Werner Muensterberger, 15–36 (New Haven, CT: Psychohistory Press, 1980).

Robbie Davis-Floyd, *Birth as an American Rite of Passage* (Berkeley: University of California Press, 1992), 8.

Tom F. Driver, *Liberating Rites; Understanding the Transformative Power of Ritual* (Boulder, CO: Westview, 1998), 166.

Clifford Geertz, *The Interpretation of Cultures* (New York: Basic Books, 1973), 5.

Sam Gill, *Native American Religious Action: A Performance Approach to Religion* (Columbia: University of South Carolina Press, 1987), 70.

Ronald L. Grimes, *Ritual Criticism: Case Studies in Its Practice, Essays on Its Theory* (Columbia: University of South Carolina Press, 1990).

Michael Houseman, "The Red and the Black: A Practical Experiment for Thinking About Ritual," in *Ritual in Its Own Right: Exploring the Dynamics of Transformation,* ed. Don Handelman and Galina Lindquist, 76 (New York: Berghahnbooks, 2005).

Richard Schechner, *Essays on Performance Theory, 1970–1976* (New York: Drama Book Specialists, 1977), 71.

Stanley J. Tambiah, *Magic, Science and Scope of Rationality* (New York: Cambridge University Press, 1990), 81.

Victor Turner, *The Forest of Symbols: Aspects of Ndembu Ritual* (Ithaca, NY: Cornell University Press, 1967), 392.

Anthony Wallace, *Religion: An Anthropological View* (New York: Random House, 1966), 107.

Chapter 5

Catherine Bell, *Ritual: Perspectives and Dimensions* (New York: Oxford University Press, 1997), ix.

Catherine Bell, *Ritual Theory, Ritual Practice* (New York: Oxford University Press, 1992), 141.

Michael Stausberg, "Ritual: A Lexicographic Survey," in *Theorizing Rituals: Issues, Topics, Approaches, Concepts,* ed. Jens Kreniath et al., 54 (Leiden: Brill, 2006).

Victor Turner, *The Forest of Symbols: Aspects of Ndembu Ritual* (Ithaca, NY: Cornell University Press 1967), 19.

Ludwig Wittgenstein, *Philosophical Investigations* (London: Blackwell, 1958), par. 66.

Chapter 6

J. L. Austin, *How to Do Things with Words,* 2nd ed. (Cambridge, MA: Harvard University Press, 1975), 5–6, 12.

Catherine Bell, *Ritual Theory, Ritual Practice* (New York: Oxford University Press, 1992), 99.

Michel Foucault, *The Hermeneutics of the Subject* (New York: Picador, 2005), 15.

Yoel Hoffmann, *The Sound of the One Hand: 281 Zen kōans with Answers* (New York: Basic Books, 1975). 47.

Edmund Leach, *The Essential Edmund Leach: Anthropology and Society* (New Haven, CT: Yale University Press, 2001), 168.

Claude Levi-Strauss, *Structural Anthropology* (New York: Basic Books, 2008), 180.

Richard Schechner, *Performance Theory* (New York: Routledge, 2003), 129–30, 322.

Zeami, *On the Art of the No Drama: The Major Treatises of Zeami,* trans. J. Thomas Rimer and Masakazu Yamazaki (Princeton, NJ: Princeton University Press, 1984), 157.

Chapter 7

Guy Debord, *The Society of the Spectacle* (New York: Zone Books 1995), 113.

Mircea Eliade, *Rites and Symbols of Initiation* (New York: Harper Torchbook 1958), 16.

Ivan Illich, *Tools for Conviviality* (New York: Marion Boyers, 1973), 11–23.

Georg Simmel, "The Sociology of Sociability," in *Theories of Society*, ed. Talcott Parsons, 158–59 (New York: Free Press of Glencoe, 1961).

Charles Taylor, *A Secular Age* (Cambridge, MA: Belknap Press, 2007), 482–83, 613.

Further reading

Should readers wish to continue their study of ritual, the selection of titles below offers a starting point into the vast literature on the subject:

Bell, Catherine. *Ritual: Perspectives and Dimensions*. New York: Oxford University Press, 1997.

Burkert, Walter. *Homo Necans: The Anthropology of Ancient Greek Sacrificial Ritual and Myth*. Translated by Peter Bing. Berkeley: University of California Press, 1983.

Driver, Tom F. *Liberating Rites: Understanding the Transformative Power of Ritual*. Boulder, CO: Westview Press, 1998.

Eliade, Mircea. *Rites and Symbols of Initiation: The Mysteries of Birth and Rebirth*. New York: Harper, 1958.

Grimes, Ronald L. *The Craft of Ritual Studies*. New York: Oxford University Press, 2013.

Grimes, Ronald L. *Deeply Into the Bone: Reinventing Rites of Passage*. Berkeley: University of California Press, 2000.

Handelman, Don, and Galina Lindquist, eds. *Ritual in Its Own Right: Exploring the Dynamics of Transformation*. New York: Berghahn Books, 2005.

Humphrey, Caroline, and James Laidlaw. *The Archetypal Actions of Ritual: A Theory of Ritual Illustrated by the Jain Rite of Worship*. New York: Oxford University Press, 1994.

Hüsken, Ute, and Frank Neubert, eds. *Negotiating Rites*. New York: Oxford University Press, 2012.

Muir, Edward. *Ritual in Early Modern Europe*. New York: Cambridge University Press, 1997.

Rappaport, Roy. *Ritual and Religion in the Making of Humanity*. New York: Cambridge University Press, 1999.

Seligman, Adam, et al. *Ritual and Its Consequences: An Essay on the Limits of Sincerity*. New York: Oxford University Press, 2008.

Smith, Jonathan Z. *To Take Place: Toward Theory in Ritual*. Chicago: University of Chicago Press, 1987.

Stephenson, Barry. *Performing the Reformation: Public Ritual in the City of Luther*. New York: Oxford University Press, 2010.

Turner, Victor. *The Ritual Process: Structure and Anti-Structure*. New York: Aldine de Gruyter, 1969.

van Gennep, Arnold. *The Rites of Passage*. Translated by Monika B. Vizedom and Gabrielle L. Caffee. Chicago, 1960 [1908].

Ritual

Index

Ritual

T

Tambiah, Stanley, 68–69
Tsembaga, pig festival of,
    17–18
Turner, Victor, 40, 59, 72–73,
    100
  distinction between ritual
    and ceremony, 71–72
Tylor, E. B., 64

V

van Gennep, Arnold, 57–58
von Frisch, Max, 7

Z

Zeami, 89
Zen kōans, 89–91